I discovered for myself and by myself that there is no self to realize.
It comes as a shattering blow.
It hits you like a thunderbolt.
You have invested everything in one basket: self-realization,
and, in the end, suddenly you discover that there is no self to discover,
no self to realize – and you say to yourself,
"What the hell have I been doing all my life?"

Contents

UNIQUE   *5*

MYSTIQUE   *12*

NOTHING   *25*

MEANING   *41*

SILENCE   *79*

EXTRAORDINARY   *95*

BELIEF   *111*

ANSWER   *130*

1

UNIQUE

UNIQUE

By some stroke of luck, or by grace of God if you will, I have come by or stumbled into a new state of being. Rather I would say, I find myself awakened to a whole new way of life.

My payer used to be, "Oh God, if there is a God, why hast Thou forsaken me?" It has now only changed into something like this: "Oh God, if there is a God…" That bit "if there is a God" still remains unchanged. "Why hast Thou chosen to bestow all Thy divine favors on me?"

But to describe in such terms as illumination, enlightenment or even by the Sanskrit word "moksha" or liberation; or even to use those fanciful words: "first and last freedom," "radical mutation," is to miss the point.

It isn't a revealed religious truth, or even, what we refer to as one beyond human intellect. There isn't anything mysterious about it. It is not what people talk of. As the spiritual apprehension of truth is intellectually incomprehensible.

There is nothing mysterious about it.

What has happened to me is a pure and simple physical phenomenon. Somehow, the machinations of the mind have come to a stop. And the senses have started functioning or operating in a pure and simple way. That, itself, is an extraordinary thing.

It is not a question of enlightenment, spiritually or intellectually, or in any form. Or to use that vulgar expression "get religious." There is nothing to get converted to any belief, or to any monastic state, or even to sit rapt in meditation seeking absorption into God or the Infinite or whatever you call it.

It isn't a tale imagining or accounting a world in which ourselves do not exist. It isn't any inexplicable affair. It is an explicable affair. There isn't anything to make a mystery of This.

If any such thing happens to an individual, he's not concerned with direct communion of the soul with God or any such thing.

Then what then is the effect of This on the conduct of an individual? It affects not only the conduct of the individual but the totality of the human being.

It is bound to affect others too. As the saying goes, "You cannot light a candle and hide it under the bushel."

What do I think of Krishnamurti?

His state of being...it being...cannot be different from that of those of the sages, saints, and saviors of mankind. The abstractions he throws at people is a kind of trick, as it were, to trick you into that state of mind where the mind comes to a stop, a sudden stop, and there something can happen.

But if you repeat those phrases, it becomes a mere twaddle, a drivel, gibberish. They haven't got much substance. You might as well quote the Bhagavad Gita, or the Bible, or even Koran, or any one of these scriptures that doesn't make any difference at all. If I've added one more, a new set of phrases, that's all there is to it. Why repeat those phrases? Why talk of flowers?

Where the eyes look at them and the ears listen to them, you are out of this structure once and for all. You will never ask these questions once again.

What is there behind and beneath those abstractions that Krishnamurti throws at people? Is there anything at all? As a mind view, as a mind concept, as a mind vision, as a mind image, or even as a sanguine expectation, they sound marvelous. They're very charming words.

If you really knew it, I don't think you would even want it. It is a dynamite. It isn't a thing to play with.

Do I know it?

What a question..Hah ..I really don't know. Your guess is as good as mine. If I tell you it is the same, what value has it? If I tell you it isn't the same, it has no value either. But why put these questions to ourselves?

What is the way of knowing It, whether be it his or anybody else's? You have absolutely no way of knowing it. If by some luck, you stumble into it, it would be a completely and totally bewildering and puzzling sort of affair. You won't even bother to compare it with anybody else's.

It isn't going to be the same...it isn't going to come about the way you imagine it, "spiritual awakening" or whatever you call it, isn't going to come about in the way you imagine it.

It will come about contrary to all your imaginings.

It will come about in a very simple and quite an unexpected way.

But anyway, what exactly IT is...Can you tell me what IT is that you are seeking? Or that you want it? Or that you are trying to find out? Can you tell me?

...To change the entire structure and thought of civilization isn't an easiest thing. That means the very foundations on which the superstructure of our civilization rests must be shattered. That can't be done very easily, and that can't be done without a change in our intellectual and religious outlook. And the very educational system must change.

But it's easy to say all that.

Unless an individual changes, there isn't going to be any change at all, and even that change, must be one without volition. And that requires tremendous and arduous understanding. If it were that simple, with all the descriptions we have in the Hindu and Buddhist scriptures, everyone in India would have been a great yogi. For surely we have 8 million Sadhus wandering all over the country.

UNIQUE

There are so many claimants, to what you call the spiritual enlightenment, that the result that you don't know who is actually enlightened, or who is really and genuinely an authentic soul who has this spiritual awakening. Western disciples seem to be the measure of the greatness of a spiritual teacher these days. They have tremendous following in Europe, in America, and all over the world. Trotting around the world, talking to these people, has become very fashionable.

2

MYSTIQUE

WHO WAS U.G.?

Whatever you do in the pursuit of truth or reality takes you away from your own very natural state in which you always are. It's not something you can acquire, attain or accomplish as a result of your effort. All that you do makes it impossible for what already is there to express itself. That is why I call this your natural state. You're always in that state. What prevents what is there from expressing itself in its own way is the search. The search is *always* in the wrong direction, so *all* that you consider very profound, *all* that you consider sacred, is a contamination in that consciousness. You may not [Laughs] like the word contamination but all that you consider *sacred, holy and profound* is a contamination. There's nothing that you can do, it's not in your hands. This is something which I can't give because you *have* it. It is ridiculous to ask for a thing which you already have. There isn't anything to get from anybody. You have what I have. I say you are there.

I was brought up in a very religious atmosphere. My grandfather was a very cultured man. He knew Blavatsky [the founder of the

MYSTIQUE

Theosophical Society] and Olcott, and then, later on, the second and third generations of Theosophists. They all visited our house. He was a great lawyer, a very rich man, a very cultured man and, very strangely, a very orthodox man. He was a sort of mixed-up kid: orthodoxy, tradition on one side and then the opposite, Theosophy and the whole thing on the other side. He failed to establish a balance. That was the beginning of my problem.

He had learned men on his payroll and he dedicated himself for some reason—I don't want to go into the whole business—to create a profound atmosphere for me and to educate me in the right way, inspired by the Theosophists and the whole lot. And so, every morning those fellows would come and read the Upanishads, Panchadasi, Nyshkarmya Siddhi, the commentaries, the commentaries on commentaries, the whole lot, from four o'clock to six o'clock, and this little boy of five, six or seven years—I don't know—had to listen to all that crap. So much so that by the time I reached my seventh year I could repeat most of those things, the passages from the Panchadasi, Nyshkarmya Siddhi and this, that and the other.

So many holy men visited my house—the Ramakrishna Order and the others; you name it, and those fellows had somehow visited that house—that was an open house for every holy man. So, one thing I discovered when I was quite young was that they were all hypocrites: they said something, they believed something, and their lives were shallow, nothing. I lived in the midst of people who talked of these things everlastingly—everybody was false, I can tell you. So somehow, what you call existentialist nausea—revulsion against everything sacred and everything holy—crept into my system and threw everything out.

That was the beginning of my search. I did everything, all the austerities. I was so young but I was determined to find out if there was any such thing as enlightenment. I wanted that very much. Otherwise, I wouldn't have given my life. Then my real search began. All my religious background was there in me. Then I started exploring. For some years I studied psychology and also philosophy, Eastern and Western, mysticism, all the modern sciences, everything. The whole area of human knowledge I started exploring on my own.

Before my forty-ninth year I had so many powers, so many experiences, but I didn't pay any attention to them. The moment I saw someone I could see their entire past, present and future without their telling me anything. I didn't use them. I was wondering, puzzled, you see, "Why do I have this power?" Sometimes I said things and they always happened. I couldn't figure out the mechanism of that. I tried to. They always happened. I didn't play with it. Then it had certain unpleasant consequences and created suffering for some people.

All kinds of funny things happened to me. I remember when I rubbed my body like this, there was a sparkle, like a phosphorous glow, on the body. She [Valentine] used to run out of her bedroom to see—she thought there were cars going that way in the middle of the night. Every time I rolled in my bed there was a sparkling of light [Laughs] and it was so funny for me—"What is this?" It was electricity—that is why I say it is an electromagnetic field. At first I thought it was because of my nylon clothes and

MYSTIQUE

static electricity; but then I stopped using nylon. I was a very skeptical heretic, to the tips of my toes, I never believed in anything; even if I saw some miracle happen before me, I didn't accept that at all—such was the make-up of this man. It never occurred to me that anything of that sort was in the making for me.

Very strange things happened to me, but I never related those things to liberation or freedom or moksha, because by that time the whole thing had gone out of my system. I had arrived at a point where I said to myself "Buddha deluded himself and deluded others. All those teachers and saviors of mankind were damned fools—they fooled themselves—so I'm not interested in this kind of thing anymore," so it went out of my system completely. It went on and on in its own way—peculiar things—but never did I say to myself, "Well, [Laughs] I am getting there, I am nearer to that." There is no nearness to that, there is no farawayness from that, there is no closeness to that. Nobody is nearer to that because he is different, he is prepared. There's no readiness for that; it just hits you like a ton of bricks.

The whole thing is finished for me and that's all. The linking gets broken and once it is broken it is finished. Then it is not once that thought explodes—every time a thought arises it explodes. The division cannot stay there, it's a physical impossibility. You don't have to do a thing about it. That is why I say that when this explosion takes place (I use the word explosion because it's like a nuclear explosion) it leaves behind chain-reactions. Every cell in your body has to undergo this change.

It's an irreversible change. There's no question of your going back. It is like a nuclear explosion. It shatters the whole body. It is not an easy thing. It is the end of the man, such a shattering thing that it blasts every cell, every nerve in your body. I went through terrible physical torture at that moment; not that you experience the explosion—you can't experience the explosion—but its after-effects. The fallout is the thing that changes the whole chemistry of your body. The senses are operating now without any coordinator or center, that's all I can say. Unless that alchemy or change in the whole chemistry takes place, there is no way of freeing this organism from thought, from the continuity of thought.

The blinking of the eyes stopped and then there were changes in taste, smell and hearing. I noticed that my skin was soft like silk and had a peculiar kind of glow, a golden color.

I no longer spend time in reverie, worry, conceptualization and the other kinds of thinking that most people do when they're alone. My mind is only engaged when it's needed, for instance when you ask questions, or when I have to fix the tape-recorder or something like that. My memory is in the background and only comes into play when it's needed, automatically. When it's not needed there is no mind here, there is no thought; there is only life.

My body had gone away and it has never come back. The points of contact are all that is there for the body. Nothing else is there for me because the seeing is altogether independent of the sense of touch here. I had discovered that all my senses were without any coordination. I felt the life energy drawing to a focal point from different parts of my body. Even now it happens to me. The hands and feet become cold, the body becomes stiff, the heartbeat slows down, the breathing slows down and then there is a gasping for breath. Up to a point you are there. You breathe your last breath, as it were, and then you are finished.

What happens after that, nobody knows. How long it lasted I don't know. I can't say anything about that because the experiencer was finished. There was nobody to experience that death at all. So that was the end of it. I got up. The things that had astonished me that week had become permanent fixtures. I call all these events a calamity because from the point of view of one who thinks this is something fantastic, blissful, full of love, ecstasy and all that kind of a thing, this is physical torture. Not a calamity to me but to those who have an image that something marvelous is going to happen.

It's something like you imagine New York. You dream about it. You want to be there. When you are actually there, nothing of it is there. It is a godforsaken place and even the devils have probably forsaken that place. It's not the thing that you had sought after and wanted so much but totally different.

What is there you really don't know. You have no way of knowing anything about that. There is no image here. Then suddenly, there was an outburst of tremendous energy shaking the whole body, vibrating. It lasted for hours. I couldn't bear it but there was nothing I could do to stop it. There was a total helplessness. This went on and on, day after day. Whenever I sat, it started—this vibration like an epileptic fit or something. Not even an epileptic fit; it went on for days. It was a very painful process because the body has limitations. It has a form, a shape of its own.

So when there is an outburst of energy which is not your energy or my energy but God's (call it by any name you like) it is like a river in spate. The energy that is operating there does not feel the limitations of the body. It is not interested. It has its own momentum. It is a very painful thing. It is not ecstatic, blissful and all that rubbish, stuff and nonsense. It is really a painful thing.

Oh I suffered for months before and after that, everybody has—a great cascade; not one but thousands. It went on and on for months. It's a very painful experience, painful in the sense that the energy has a peculiar operation of its own. It is clockwise, counterclockwise, and then it is this way, and then this way, and then this way. Like an atom, it moves inside—not in one part of your body—the whole body. It is as if a wet towel were being wrung to get rid of the water. It is like that—the whole of our body. It's such a painful thing. It goes on even now. You can't invite it. You can't ask it to come. You can't do anything. It gives you the feeling that it is enveloping you, that it is descending on you.

Every time it is new. Very strange, every time it comes in a different way. So you don't know what is happening. You lie down on your bed and suddenly it begins. It begins to move slowly like ants. I'd think there were bugs in my bed, jump out, look, see no bugs, then I'd go back, then again. The hairs are electrified. So it slowly moves. There were pains all over the body. Thought has controlled this body to such an extent that when that loosens, the whole metabolism is agog. The whole thing was changing in its own way without my doing anything. Every cell started changing and it went on and on for six months. In all, it took three years for this body to fall into a new rhythm of its own. I behaved normally, I didn't know what was happening. It was a strange situation.

The state is something natural. Do you see the swellings here? Yesterday was the new moon. The body is affected by everything that is happening around you. It is not separate. Whatever is happening there is also happening here. There is only the physical response. This is affection. Your body is affected by everything that is happening around you, and you can't prevent this for the simple reason that the armor that you have built around yourself is destroyed. So it is very vulnerable to everything that is happening there.

There are certain glands. These ductless glands are located in exactly the same spots where the Hindus speculated the chakras are. They have feelings, extraordinary feelings. There is one gland here which is called the thymus gland. Doctors tell us that is active through childhood until puberty then becomes dormant. In your natural state that gland is reactivated.

If somebody hurts himself there, that hurt is felt here—not as a pain, but there is a feeling, you see—you automatically say "Ah!" This actually happened to me when I was staying in a coffee plantation: a mother started beating a child, a little child, you know. She was mad, hopping mad, and she hit the child so hard, the child almost turned blue. And somebody asked me "Why did you not interfere and stop her?" I was standing there—I was so puzzled, you see. "Who should I take pity on, the mother or the child?"—that was my answer—"Who is responsible?" Both were in a ridiculous situation: the mother could not control her anger, and the child was so helpless and innocent. This went on—it was moving from one to the other—and then I found all those things [marks] on my back. So I was also part of that. (I am not saying this just to claim something.) That is possible because consciousness cannot be divided. Anything that is happening there is affecting you—this is affection, you understand? There is no question of your sitting in judgement on anybody; the situation happens to be that, so you are affected by that. You are affected by everything that is happening there.

Consciousness is, of course, not limited. If he is hurt there, you also are hurt here. If you are hurt, there is an immediate response there. I can't say about the universe, the whole universe, but in your field of consciousness, in the limited field in which you are operating at that particular moment, you are responding—not that you are responding.

And all the other glands also here... There are so many glands here; for example, the pituitary—'third eye', 'ajna [command] chakra', they call it. When once the interference of thought is finished, it is taken over by this gland: it is this gland that gives the instructions or orders to the body; not thought any more; thought cannot interfere. (That is why they call it that, probably. I'm not interpreting or any such thing; perhaps this gives you an idea.) But you have built an armor created an armor with this thought, and you don't allow yourself to be affected by things. But you have built an armor, created an armor, with this thought and you don't allow yourself to be affected by things.

MYSTIQUE

Since there is nobody who uses this thought as a self-protective mechanism it burns itself up. Thought undergoes combustion—ionization, if I may use your scientific term. Thought is, after all, vibration. When this kind of ionization of thought takes place it sometimes covers the whole body with an ash-like substance. Your body is covered with that when there is no need for thought at all. When you don't use it what happens to that thought? It burns itself out—that is the energy—it's a combustion. The body gets heated, you know. There is tremendous heat in the body as a result of this, and so the skin is covered—your face, your feet, everything—with this ash-like substance. That's one of the reasons why I express it in pure and simple physical and physiological terms. It has no psychological content at all. It has no mystical content. It has no religious overtones at all, as I see it. I am bound to say that and I don't care whether you accept it or not. It is of no importance to me.

This kind of a thing must have happened to so many people. It is not something that one is specially prepared for. There are no purificatory methods necessary. There is no spiritual practice necessary for this kind of a thing to happen, no preparation of any kind. The consciousness is so pure that whatever you are doing in the direction of purifying that consciousness is adding impurity to it. Consciousness has to flush itself out, it has to purge itself of every trace of holiness, every trace of unholiness, everything. Even what you consider sacred and holy is a contamination in that consciousness.

It is not through any volition of yours. When once the frontiers are broken—not through any effort of yours, not through any volition of yours—then the floodgates are open and everything goes out. In that process of flushing out you have all these visions. It's not a vision outside there or inside of you. Suddenly, your whole consciousness takes the shape of those people who have come into this state. Not great men, not the leaders of mankind, it is very strange, but only those people to whom this kind of a thing happened.

3

NOTHING

NOTHING

U.G.: You see, I maintain that -- I don't know, whatever you call this; I don't like to use the words 'enlightenment,' 'freedom,' *'moksha'* or 'liberation'; all these words are loaded words, they have a connotation of their own -- this cannot be brought about through any effort of yours; it just happens. And why it happens to one individual and not another, I don't know.

Questioner: So, it happened to you?

U.G.: It happened to me.

Q: When, Sir?

U.G.: In my forty-ninth year.

But whatever you do in the direction of whatever you are after -- the pursuit or search for truth or reality -- takes you away from your own very natural state, in which you *always* are. It's not something you can acquire, attain or accomplish as a result of your effort -- that is why I use the word `acausal'. It has no cause, but somehow the search come to an end.

Q: You think, Sir, that it is not the result of the search? I ask because I have heard that you studied philosophy, that you were associated with religious people ...

U.G.: You see, the search takes you away from yourself -- it is in the opposite direction -- it has absolutely no relation.

Q: In spite of it, it has happened, not because of it?

U.G.: *In spite* of it -- yes, that's the word. All that you do makes it impossible for what already is there to express itself. That is why I call this 'your natural state'. You're always in that state. What prevents what is there from expressing itself in its own way is the search. The search is *always* in the wrong direction, so *all* that you consider very profound, *all* that you consider sacred, is a contamination in that consciousness. You may not (Laughs) like the word 'contamination', but all that you consider *sacred, holy* and *profound* is a contamination.

So, there's nothing that you can do. It's not in your hands. I don't like to use the word 'grace', because if you use the word 'grace', the grace of whom? You are not a specially chosen individual; you deserve this, I don't know why.

If it were possible for me, I would be able to help *somebody*. This is something which I *can't give*, because you *have* it. Why should I give it to you? It is ridiculous to ask for a thing which you already have.

Q: But I don't feel it, and you do.

U.G.: *No,* it is not a question of feeling it, it is not a question of knowing it; you will never *know.* You have no way of knowing that at all for yourself; it begins to express itself. There is no conscious... You see, I don't know how to put it. Never does the thought that I am different from anybody come into my consciousness.

Q: Has it been so from the beginning, ever since you became conscious of yourself?

U.G.: No, I can't say that. I was after something -- like anybody else brought up in the religious atmosphere -- searching for something, pursuing something. So, to answer that question is not easy, because I'll have to go into the whole background. Maybe it comes, I don't know. (Laughs)

Q: Just out of curiosity, like Nachiketa, I am very interested in knowing how these things have happened to you personally, to the extent you are aware of.

U.G.: You see, that's a long story; it's not so simple.

Q: We would like to hear it.

U.G.: No, you see, I will have to tell you about my whole life -- it will take me a long time. My life story goes up to a point, and then it stops -- there is no more biography after that.

The two biographers who are interested in writing my biography have two different approaches. One says that what I did -- the *sadhana* (spiritual exercises), education, the whole background -- put me there. I say it was in spite of all that. (Laughter) The other biographer isn't much interested in my statement 'in spite of', because there isn't much material for him to write a big volume. (Laughter) They are more interest in that. The publishers too are interested in that kind of thing. That is very natural because you are operating in a field where the cause and effect relationship always operates -- that is why you are interested in finding out the cause, how this kind of a thing happened. So, we are back where we started, square number one: we are still concerned with 'how'.

My background is *worthless:* it can't be a model for anybody, because your background is unique. Every event in your life is something unique in its own way. Your conditions, your environment, your background -- the whole thing is different. Every event in your life is different.

Q: I don't seek a model to give to the rest of the world -- I'm not asking from that angle. We see a star, we see the sun, we see the moon -- it is like that; not that I would like to imitate you. It may be relevant, who knows? That is why I said I am Nachiketa here: I don't want to leave without knowing the truth from you.

NOTHING

U.G.: You need a Yama Dharmaraja to answer your questions.

Q: If you don't mind, you be Yama Dharmaraja.

U.G.: I don't mind. Help me. You see, I'm helpless, I don't know where to begin. Where to end, I know. (Laughter) I think I will have to tell the whole story of my life.

Q: We don't mind listening.

U.G.: It doesn't come.

Q: You need to be inspired.

U.G.: I am not inspired, and I am the last person to inspire anybody. I will have to tell you, to satisfy your curiosity, the other side, the shoddy side of my life.

(He was born 9 July 1918 in South India into an upper-middle-class Brahmin family. The family name being Uppaluri, he was given the name Uppaluri Gopala Krishnamurti. His mother died soon after his birth, and he was brought up by his maternal grandparents in the small town of Gudivada near Masulipatam.)

I was brought up in a very religious atmosphere. My grandfather was a very cultured man. He knew Blavatsky (the founder of the Theosophical Society) and Olcott, and then, later on, the second and third generation of Theosophists. They all visited our house. He was a great lawyer, a very rich man, a very cultured man and, very strangely, a very orthodox man. He was a sort of mixed-up kid: orthodoxy, tradition on one side, and then the opposite,

Theosophy and the whole thing, on the other side. He failed to establish a balance. That was the beginning of my problem.

(UG was often told that his mother had said, just before she died, that he "was born to a destiny immeasurably high." His grandfather took this very seriously and gave up his law practice to devote himself to UG's upbringing and education. His grandparents and their friends were convinced that he was a *yoga bhrashta,* one who had come within inches of enlightenment in his past life.)

He had learned men on his pay-roll, and he dedicated himself, for some reason -- I don't want to go into the whole business -- to create a profound atmosphere for me and to educate me in the right way, inspired by the Theosophists and the whole lot. And so, every morning those fellows would come and read the Upanishads, *Panchadasi, Nyshkarmya Siddhi,* the commentaries, the commentaries on commentaries, the whole lot, from four o'clock to six o'clock, and this little boy of five, six or seven years -- I don't know -- had to listen to all that crap. So much so that by the time I reached my seventh year I could repeat most of those things, the passages from the Panchadasi, Nyshkarmya Siddhi and this, that and the other. So many holy men visited my house -- the Ramakrishna Order and the others; you name it, and those fellows had somehow visited that house -- that was an open house for every holy man. So, one thing I discovered when I was quite young was that they were all hypocrites: they said something, they believed something, and their lives were shallow, *nothing.* That was the beginning of my search.

My grandfather used to meditate. (He is dead, and I don't want to say anything bad about him.) He used to meditate for one or two hours in a separate meditation room. One day a little baby, one and a half or two years old, started crying for some reason. That chap came down and started beating the child, and the child almost turned blue -- and this man, you see, meditating two hours every day. "Look! What is this he has done?" That posed a sort of (I don't want to use the psychological term, but there is no escape from it) a traumatic experience -- "There must be something funny about the whole business of meditation. Their lives are shallow, empty. They talk marvelously, express things in a very beautiful way, but what about their lives? There is this neurotic fear in their lives: they say something, but it doesn't operate in their lives. What is wrong with them?" -- not that I sat in judgement over those people.

Things went on and on and on, so I got involved with these things: "Is there anything to what they profess -- the Buddha, Jesus, the great teachers? Everybody is talking about *moksha*, liberation, freedom. What is that? I want to know for myself. These are all useless fellows, yet there must be some person in this world who is an embodiment and apostle of all those things. If there is one, I want to find out for myself."

Then so many things happened. There was one man called Sivananda Saraswati in those days -- he was the evangelist of Hinduism. Between the ages of fourteen and twenty- one (I am skipping many of the unnecessary events) I used to go there and meet him very often, and I did everything, all the austerities. I was so young, but I was determined to find out if there was any such thing as *moksha,* and I wanted that *moksha* for myself. I wanted to prove to myself and to everybody that there cannot be any hypocrisy in such people -- "These are all hypocrites" -- so I practiced yoga, I practiced meditation, studied everything. I experienced every kind of experience that the books talked about -- *samadhi,* super-*samadhi, nirvikalpa samadhi,* everything. Then I said to myself "Thought can create *any* experience you want -- bliss, beatitude, ecstasy, melting away into nothingness -- all those experiences. So, this can't be the thing, because I'm the same person, mechanically doing these things. Meditations have no value for me. This is not leading me anywhere."

Then, you see, sex became a tremendous problem for me, a young human boy: "This is something natural, a biological thing, an urge in the human body. Why do these people all want to deny this sex and suppress something very natural, something which is part of the whole thing, in order to get something else? This is more real, more important to me than *moksha* and liberation and all that. This is a reality -- I think of gods and goddesses and I have wet-dreams -- I have this kind of a thing. Why should I feel guilty? It's something natural; I have no control over this kind of thing happening. Meditation has not helped me, study has not helped me, my disciplines have not helped me. I never touch salt, I never touch chilies or any spices." Then one day I found this man Sivananada eating mango pickles behind closed doors -- "Here is a man who has denied himself everything in the hope of getting something, but that fellow cannot control himself. He is a hypocrite" -- I don't want to say anything bad about him -- "This kind of life is not for me."

Q: Between your fourteenth and twenty-first year, you say, you felt a great urge for sex. Did you marry then?

U.G.: No, I didn't rush; I allowed that. I wanted to experience the sex urge: "Suppose you don't do anything, what happens to that?" I wanted to understand this whole business: "Why do I want to indulge in these auto-eroticisms? I don't know anything about sex -- then, why is it that I have all kinds of images of sex?" This was my inquiry, this was my meditation; not sitting in lotus posture or standing on my head. "How am I able to form these images?" -- I never went to a movie, I never looked at, you know, now you have all kinds of posters --"How is it? This is something inside, not put in from outside. The outside is stimulating -- stimulation comes from outside. But there is another kind of stimulation from inside -- this is more important to me. I can cut out all that external stimulation successfully, but how can I cut out this from inside?" I wanted to find this out.

And then, I was also interested in finding out what this sex experience was. Although I myself had not experienced sex, I seemed to know what that sex experience was like. This went on and on and on. I did not rush to have sex with a woman or anything; I allowed things to happen in their own way. That was a time when I didn't want to marry. My aim was to become an ascetic, a monk, and all that kind of thing -- not marriage -- but things happened and I said to myself "If it is a question of satisfying your sex urge, why not marry? That is what society is there for. Why should you go and have sex with some woman? You can have a natural expression of sex in marriage."

WHO WAS U.G.?

I arrived at a point when I was twenty-one where I felt very strongly that all teachers -- Buddha, Jesus, Sri Ramakrishna, everybody -- kidded themselves, deluded themselves and deluded everybody. This, you see, could not be the thing at all -- "Where is the state that these people talk about and describe? That description seems to have no relation to me, to the way I am functioning. Everybody says "Don't get angry" --- I am angry all the time. I'm full of brutal activities inside, so that is false. What these people are telling me I should be is something false, and because it is false it will falsify me. I don't want to live the life of a false person. I am greedy, and non-greed is what they are talking about. There is something wrong somewhere. This greed is something real, something natural to me; what they are talking about is unnatural. So, something is wrong somewhere. But I am not ready to change myself, to falsify myself, for the sake of being in a state of non-greed; my greed is a reality to me." I lived in the midst of people who talked of these things everlastingly -- everybody was false, I can tell you. So, somehow, what you call 'existentialist nausea' (I didn't use those words at the time, but now I happen to know these terms, revulsion against everything sacred and everything holy, crept into my system and threw everything out: "No more *slokas*, no more religion, no more practices -- there isn't anything there; but what is here is something natural. I am a brute, I am a monster, I am full of violence -- this is reality. I am full of desire. Desirelessness, non-greed, non-anger -- those things have no meaning to me; they are false, and they are not only false, they are falsifying me." So I said to myself "I'm finished with the whole business," but it is not that simple, you see.

Then somebody came along, and we were discussing all these things. He found me practically an atheist (but not a practicing atheist), skeptical of everything, heretical down to my boots. He said "There is one man here, somewhere in Madras at Tiruvannamalai, called Ramana Maharshi. Come on, let's go and see that man. Here is a living human embodiment of the Hindu tradition."

I didn't want to see any holy man. If you have seen one, you have seen them all. I never shopped around, went around searching for people, sitting at the feet of the masters, learning something; because everybody tells you "Do more and more of the same thing, and you will get it." What I got were more and more experiences, and then those experiences demanded permanence -- and there is no such thing as permanence. So, "The holy men are all phonies -- they are telling me only what is there in the books. That I can read -- 'Do the same again and again' -- that I don't want. Experiences I don't want. They are trying to share an experience with me. I'm not interested in experience. As far as experience goes, for me there is no difference between the religious experience and the sex experience or any other experience; the religious experience is like any other experience. I am not interested in experiencing *Brahman;* I am not interested in experiencing reality; I am not interested in experiencing truth. They might help others; but they cannot help me. I'm not interested in doing more of the same; what I have done is enough. At school if you want to solve a mathematical problem, you repeat it again and again -- you solve the mathematical problem, and you discover that the answer is in the problem. So, what the hell are you doing, trying to solve the problem? It is easier to find the answer first instead of going through all this."

So, reluctantly, hesitatingly, unwilling, I went to see Ramana Maharshi. That fellow dragged me. He said "Go there once. Something will happen to you." He talked about it and gave me a book, *Search in Secret India* by Paul Brunton, so I read the chapter relating to this man -- "All right, I don't mind, let me go and see." That man was sitting there. From his very presence I felt "What! This man -- how can he help me? This fellow who is reading comic strips, cutting vegetables, playing with this, that or the other -- how can this man help me? He can't help me." Anyway, I sat there. Nothing *happened;* I looked at him, and he looked at me. "In his presence you feel silent, your questions disappear, his look changes you" -- all that remained a story, fancy stuff to me. I sat there. There were a lot of questions inside, silly questions -- so, "The questions have not disappeared. I have been sitting here for two hours, and the questions are still there. All right, let me ask him some questions" -- because at that time I very much wanted *moksha*. This part of my background, *moksha*, I wanted. "You are supposed to be a liberated man" -- I didn't say that. "Can you give me what you have?" -- I asked him this question, but that man didn't answer, so after some lapse of time I repeated that question -- "I am asking 'Whatever you have, can you give it to me?'" He said, "I can give you, but can you *take* it?" Boy! For the first time this fellow says that he has something and that I can't take it. Nobody before had said "I can give you," but this man said "I can give you, but can you take it?" Then I said to myself "If there is any individual in this world who can take it, it is me, because I have done so much *sadhana*, seven years of *sadhana*. He can think that I can't take it, but I can take it. If I can't take it, who can take it?" - -- that was my frame of mind at the time -- you know, (Laughs) I was so confident of myself.

I didn't stay with him, I didn't read any of his books, so I asked him a few more questions: "Can one be free sometimes and not free sometimes?" He said "Either you are free, or you are not free at all." There was another question which I don't remember. He answered in a very strange way: "There are no steps leading you to that." But I ignored all these things. These questions didn't matter to me -- the answers didn't interest me at all.

But this question "Can you take it?" ... "How arrogant he is!" -- that was my feeling. "Why can't I take it, whatever it is? What is it that he has?" -- that was my question, a natural question. So, the question formulated itself: "What is that state that all those people - - Buddha, Jesus and the whole gang -- were in? Ramana is in that state -- supposed to be, I don't know -- but that chap is like me, a human being. How is he different from me? What others say or what he is saying is of no importance to me; anybody can do what he is doing. What is there? He can't be very much different from me. He was also born from parents. He has his own particular ideas about the whole business. Some people say something happened to him, but how is he different from me? What is there: *What is that state?*" -- that was my fundamental question, the basic question -- that went on and on and on. "I must find out what that state is. Nobody can give that state; I am on my own. I have to go on this uncharted sea without a compass, without a boat, with not even a raft to take me. I am going to find out for myself what the state is in which that man is." I wanted that very much, otherwise I wouldn't have given my life.

Q: This giving-taking business, I don't understand.

U.G.: I can't say anything about what he meant when he said "I can give it, but can you take it?" but in a way that helped me to formulate my own question. You see, if somebody were to ask me a similar question now, I would say there isn't anything to get from anybody. Who am I to give it to you? You have what I have. We are all at 25 Sannidhi Street, and you are asking me "Where is 25 Sannidhi Street?" I say you are there. Not that I know I am there. This wanting to know where you are -- you are asking that question.

4

MEANING

U.G.: You will never be free from selfishness.

Q: But all the saints, saviors and religions of all times have encouraged us to be unselfish, to be self-effacing, to be meek. It must therefore be possible. How can you be so certain of such a thing?

U.G.: Because it is crystal clear to me that you have invented this idea of selflessness to protect yourself from the actual -- your selfishness. In any case, whether you believe in selflessness or not, you remain at all times selfish. Your so-called selflessness exists only in the future, tomorrow. And when tomorrow comes, it is put off until the next day, or perhaps next life.

Look at it this way; it is like the horizon. Actually, there is no horizon. The more you move towards the horizon, the more it moves away. It is only the limitations of the eyes that creates the horizon. But there is no such thing as the horizon. Likewise, there is no such thing as selflessness at all. Man has tortured himself for generations with this idea of selflessness, and it has only afforded a living for those who sell the idea of selflessness for a living, like the priests and moralists.

I am not condemning you or anyone else, just pointing out the absurdity of what you are doing.

When the energy that is spent in the pursuit of something that does not exist, like selflessness, is released, your problem becomes very simple, no matter what it is. You will cease to create problems on the material plane, and that's the only plane there is.

Q: Yes, but what about those who are not searching for some illusory abstraction, but simply happiness?

U.G.: Their search for happiness is no different from the spiritual pursuit. It is the pursuit of pleasure, spirituality being the greatest, ultimate pleasure.

Q: So this pursuit has to go?

U.G.: Don't say it should go. Wanting selfishness to go is part and parcel of the selfish pursuit of a more pleasurable state -- selflessness. Both do not exist. That is why you are eternally unhappy. Your search for happiness is making you unhappy. Both the spiritual goal and the search for happiness are the same. Both are essentially selfish, pleasurable pursuits. If that understanding is somehow there in you, then you will not use the energy in that direction at all.

You know, I've been everywhere in the world, and have found that people are exactly the same. There is no difference at all. *Becoming* is the most important thing in the world for everybody -- to become something. They all want to become rich, whether materially or spiritually, it is exactly the same. Don't divide it; the so-called spiritual is the materialistic. You may think you are superior because you go to temple and do *puja*, but the woman there is doing *puja* in the hope of having a child. She wants something, so she goes to the temple. So do you; it is exactly the same. For sentimental reasons you go, but in time it will become routine and become abhorrent to you.

What I am trying to point out is simply this: your spiritual and religious activities are basically selfish. That is all I am pointing out. You go to the temple for the same reason you go other places -- you want some result. If you don't want anything there is no reason to go to the temple.

Q: But the great majority of people go to the temple ...

U.G.: Why are you so concerned about what the majority does? This is your problem, and you must solve it for yourself. Don't bother about mankind and all the billions of people in the world.

Q: You are ruthlessly condemning whatever people have said so far. You may, in time, also be condemned and blasted for what you are saying.

U.G.: If you have the guts, I will be the very first to salute you. But you must not rely on your holy books -- the *Bhagavad Gita*(1) or *Upanishads*. You must challenge what I am saying without the help of your so-called authorities. You just don't have the guts to do that because you are relying upon the Gita, not upon yourself. That is why you will never be able to do it. If you have that courage, you are the only person who can falsify what I am saying. A great sage like Gowdapada(2) can do it, but he is not here. You are merely repeating what Gowdapada and others have said. It is a worthless statement as far as you are concerned. If there were a living Gowdapada sitting here, he would be able to blast what I am saying, but not you. So don't escape into meaningless generalizations. You must have the guts to disprove what I am saying on your own. What I am saying must be false for you. You can only agree or disagree with what I am saying according to what some joker has told you. That is not the way to go about it.

I am just pointing out that there are no solutions at all, only problems. If others have said the same thing I am saying, why are you asking questions and searching for solutions here? Forget about the masses; I am talking about you. You are merely looking for new, better methods. I am not going to help you. I am saying, "Don't bother about solutions; try to find out what the problem is." The problem is the solution; solutions just don't solve your problem. Why in the hell are you looking for another solution? Don't come to me for solutions. That is all I am saying. You will make out of what I am saying another solution, to be added to your list of solutions, which are all useless when it comes to actually solving your problems.

MEANING

What I am saying is valid and true for me, that is all. If I suggest *anything*, directly or indirectly, you will turn it into another method or technique. I would be falsifying myself if I were to make any such suggestion.

If *anyone* says there is a way out, he is not an honest fellow. He is doing it for his own self-aggrandizement, you may be sure. He simply wants to market a product and hopes to convince you that it is superior to other products on the market. If another man comes along and says that there is no way out, you make of that another method. It is all a fruitless attempt to overtake your own shadow. And yet you can't remain where you are. *That* is the problem.

From all this you inevitably draw the conclusion that the situation is hopeless. In reality you are creating that hopelessness because you don't really want to be free from fear, envy, jealousy, and selfishness. That is why you feel your situation to be hopeless. The only hope lies in selfishness, greed, and anger, not in its fictitious opposite, i.e., the practice of selflessness, generosity, and kindness. The problem, say selfishness, is only strengthened by the cultivation of its fictitious opposite, the so-called selflessness.

Sitting here discussing these things is meaningless, useless. That is why I am always saying to my listeners, "Get lost, please!" What you want you can get elsewhere, but not here. Go to the temple, do *puja*, repeat *mantras*, put on ashes. Eventually some joker comes along and says, "Give me a week's wages and I will give you a better *mantra* to repeat." Then another fellow comes along and tells you not to do any of that, that it is useless, and that what he is saying is much more revolutionary. He prescribes "choiceless awareness," takes your money and builds schools, organizations, and tantric centers.

Q: Why shouldn't we brush aside what you are saying, just as you brush aside the teachings and efforts of others?

U.G.: You will never blast me; the attachment you have to religious authority prohibits you from questioning *anything*, much less a man like me. I am certain you will never challenge me. For that reason what I am saying will inevitably create an unstable, neurotic situation for you. You cannot accept what I am saying, and neither are you in any position to reject it. If it wasn't for your very thick skin, you would certainly end up in the loony bin. You simply cannot and will not question what I am saying; it is too much of a threat. Absolutely *nothing* is going to penetrate your defenses; Gowdapada provides the gloves, the Bhagavad Gita a snug coat jacket, and the *Brahmasutra*(3) a bullet-proof vest. So you are safe, and that is all you are really interested in. You can't blast what I am saying as long as you are relying upon what someone has said before.

Please don't say that there are thousands of seers and sages; there are only a very few. You can count them all on your fingers. The rest are merely technocrats. The saint is a technocrat. That is what most people are. But now with the development of drugs and other techniques, the saint is dispensable. You don't any longer need a priest or saint to instruct you in meditation. If you want to control your thoughts, simply take a drug and forget them, if that is what you want. If you can't sleep, take a sleeping pill. Sleep for a while, then wake up. It is the same.

Don't listen to me. It will create an unnecessary disturbance in you. It will only intensify the neurotic situation you are already caught in. Having taken for granted the validity of all this holy stuff, having never questioned, much less broken away from it, you not only have learned how to live with it, but also how to capitalize on it. It is a matter of profiteering, nothing more.

Q: If all this is so, then why do you go on talking?

U.G.: There is no use asking me why I talk. Am I selling or promising you anything? I am not offering you peace of mind, am I? You counter by saying that I am taking away your precious peace of mind. On the contrary, I am singing my own song, just going my own way, and you come along and attempt to disturb my peace.

Q: I feel that if anybody can help us it is you.

U.G.: No sir! Anything I do to help would only add to your misery -- that is all. By continuing to listen to me you merely heap one more misery upon those you already have. In that sense this discussion we are having is doing you no good whatever. You don't seem to realize that you are playing with fire here. If you really want *moksha* here and now, you can have it. You see, you ARE anger, selfishness, and all these things; if they go, you go. There is a physical going -- not in the abstract, but actual physical death.

Q: You are saying that that can happen now? Others have said ...

U.G.: I don't give a hoot what others have said. It can happen now. You simply don't want it. You would not touch it with a ten-foot barge pole. If anger and selfishness, which is YOU go, *moksha* is now, not tomorrow. Your own anger will burn you, not the electric heater. So the religious man has invented selflessness. If that selflessness goes, you go, that is all. So, freeing yourself from any one of these things (i.e., greed, selfishness, etc.,) implies that you, as you know and experience yourself, are coming to an end NOW. Please, in your interest and out of compassion I am telling you, this is not what you want. This is not a thing you can make happen. It is not in your hands at all. It hits whomsoever it chooses. You are out of the picture altogether.

All that poetry and romanticism about "dying to all your yesterdays" is not going to help you, or anybody. Nothing can come out of it. They may hold forth on platforms, but they themselves don't want it. It is just words. Eventually people settle for that (viz., temples, *mantras*, scriptures). It is all too absurd and childish.

Q: Then how can we find out for ourselves and not just repeat the words of the so-called experts?

U.G.: You have to actually touch life at a point where nobody has touched it before. Nobody can teach you that. As long as you continue to repeat what others have said before, you are lost, and nothing good can come of it. Listening to and believing what others have said is not the way to find out for yourself, and there is no other way.

Q: So you are saying that we must get rid of our belief that...

U.G.: Don't bother. You will replace one belief with another. You are nothing but belief, and when it dies, you are dead. What I am trying to tell you is this: don't try to be free from selfishness, greed, anger, envy, desire, and fear. You will only create its opposites, which are, unfortunately, fictitious. If desire dies, you die. The black van comes and carts you away, that's it! Even if you should somehow miraculously survive such a shock, it will be of *no use* to you, or to others.

You prefer to toy with things, asking absurd questions like, "What happens to my body after death? Will the body be strong enough to take it?" What the hell are you talking about? You are asking me what will happen to you if you touch that live electrical wire there. That is the kind of pointless question you are asking. You are not really interested at all. Perhaps after touching this you will be completely burnt and have to be thrown away. Perhaps others will get a shock themselves upon touching you, and you will become an untouchable!

Look at what is implied by what I am saying. If you have the courage to touch life for the first time, you will never know what hit you. Everything man has taught, felt, and experienced is gone, and nothing is put in its place. Such a person becomes the living authority by virtue of his freedom from the past, culture, and he will remain so until someone else who has discovered this for himself blasts it. Until you have the courage to blast me, all that I am saying, and all the gurus, you will remain a cultist with photographs, rituals, birthday celebrations, and the like.

I am sorry. I sing my song and go.

Q: But we are lost, and so we need gurus, *sadhana*, and scriptures or guidance.

U.G.: You can go back to your gurus. Do what you like. The thing I am talking about happens to the lucky; if you are lucky, you are lucky. That is all. I have nothing to do with it. It is in no one's hands.

Q: Lucky or unlucky, our tradition tells us that life is transient, that all is in flux, that...

U.G.: *That* is the tradition of India I am talking about -- *change*, not the tradition you talk about, which is *no change*. Your whole life is a denial of the reality of change. You only wish to continue, somehow, then revive, only to continue. That is not the great tradition of India I am talking of. You think you are asking a profound question when you ask, "What is death?" You presume to ask Gowdapada's question before you have asked the more fundamental question, "Am I born?" Instead of tackling this basic question on your own, you quote and write commentaries upon Gowdapada, then take the easy way out, and simply equate what I am saying with what he said. That is your cop out.

In any event, all you can do is to speculate about death and reincarnation. Only dead people ask about death. Those who are really living would never ask such a question. That memory in you--which is dead--wants to know if it will continue even after what it imagines to be death. That is why it is asking such silly questions. Death is finality; you are dead only once. When once the questions and ideas you have have died, then you will never ask about death again.

Q: You are ripping everything away, and suddenly I see that I have to strike out on my own, that no one can help me.

U.G.: Are you sure that no one can help you? You are not so sure. So your statement doesn't mean anything. You will harbor hope. Even assuming for a moment that an outside force can help you, you are still convinced that *you can help yourself.* This gives you tremendous hope, and hope is *always* oriented towards achieving something. So, rather than waste your time asking if there is or is not anyone who can help you achieve what you want, you should rather be asking, "Is there anything to be attained?" Whether you yourself, or someone else, helps you to attain it is not the issue at all. It is, rather, that you are searching. That is obvious. But for what are you searching? You are undoubtedly searching for what you already know. It is impossible to search for something you do not know. You search for, and find, what you know. It is difficult for you to face this simple fact.

Please don't get me wrong. I am not asking questions, playing some kind of Socratic guessing game. I am not here to offer you any new methods, new techniques, or suggest any gimmicks to attain your goal. If other systems, techniques, and gimmicks have failed to help you reach your goal, and if you are looking or shopping around for some newer, better methods here, I am afraid I cannot be of any help to you. If you feel that someone else can help you, good luck to you. But I am compelled, through the lessons of my own experience, to add the rider, "You will get nowhere, you will see."

The uselessness of turning to inner or outer sources to help you is something of which I am certain. It is clear to me that to find out for yourself you must be absolutely helpless with nowhere to turn. That is all. Unfortunately, this certainty cannot be transmitted to someone else. The certainty I have is simply that the goal, which you have invented, is responsible for your search. As long as the goal is there, so long will the search for it continue. If you say, "I really don't know what I am searching for," that is not true. So, what is it that you are searching for? That is by far the most important question to ask yourself.

If you look at it you will see that, aside from your natural physical needs, what you want has arisen from what you have been told, what you have read, and what you yourself have experienced. The physical wants are self-evident and easily understandable. But this particular want--the object of your search--is something born out of your thinking, which in turn is based upon the knowledge you have gathered from various sources.

Q: If all you say is true, we are in a bad way indeed. We are not in a position to accept or reject what you are saying. Why, then, do you go on talking to us? What meaning can it have?

MEANING

U.G.: This dialogue with you has no meaning at all. You may very well ask why the hell I am talking. I emphatically assure you that, in my case, it is not at all in the nature of self-fulfillment. My motive for talking is quite different from what you think it is. It is not that I am eager to help you understand, or that I feel that I must help you. Not at all. My motive is direct and temporary: you arrive seeking understanding, while I am only interested in making it crystal clear that *there is nothing to understand.*

As long as you want to understand, so long there will be this awkward relationship between two individuals. I am always emphasizing that somehow the truth has to dawn upon you that there is nothing to understand. As long as you think, accept, and believe that there is something to understand, and make that understanding a goal to be placed before you, demanding search and struggle, you are lost and will live in misery.

I have only a few things to say and I go on repeating them again and again and again. There are no questions for me, other than the practical questions for everyday functioning in this world. You, however, have many, many questions. These questions all have the same source: your knowledge. It is simply not in the nature of things that you can have a question without knowing the answer already. So meaningful dialogue is simply not possible when you are asking questions to yourself and to me, because you have already made up your mind, you already possess the answers. So communication between us is impossible; what is the point of carrying on any dialogue?

There is the actual need to be free from answers themselves. The search is invalid because it is based upon questions which in turn are based upon false knowledge. Your knowledge has not freed you from your problems. Your dilemma is that you are searching for answers to questions you already know the answer to. This is making you neurotic. If the questions you have were actually solvable, it, the question, would blow itself up. Because all questions are merely variations on the same question, the annihilation of one means the annihilation of all. So freedom exists not in finding answers, but in the dissolution of all questions. This sort of problem-solving you are not, unfortunately, the least interested in.

What others and you yourself think are the answers cannot help you at all. It is really very simple: if the answer is correct, the question disappears. I have no questions of any kind. They never enter my head. All my questions, which resolved themselves into one great question, have disappeared entirely. The questioner simply realized that it was meaningless to go on asking questions, the answers to which I already knew. You have foolishly created this search as an answer to your questions, which in turn have been invented out of the knowledge you have gathered. The questions you are formulating are born out of answers you already have. So what is your goal? You must be very clear about it; otherwise there is no point in proceeding. It becomes a game, a meaningless ritual.

What do you want to get? There is always somebody to help you get what you want, for a price. You have foolishly divided life into higher and lower goals, into material and spiritual paths. In either case great struggle, pain, and effort is involved. I say, on the other hand, that there are no spiritual goals at all; they are simply the extension of material goals into what you imagine to be a higher, loftier plane. You mistakenly believe that by pursuing the spiritual goal you will somehow miraculously make your material goals simple and manageable. Such pursuits are in actuality not possible. You may think that only inferior persons pursue material goals, that material achievements are boring. But in fact the so-called spiritual goals you have put before yourself are exactly the same. You are your search, and it will not help to think that you have understood and are free of this. If you don't come here, you will go elsewhere in search of answers.

Q: Discovering the reality you are talking about demands real relationship and open communication with others, does it not?

U.G.: Forget it, sir! Dialogue has no meaning. Neither has conversation any meaning. What the hell are we doing? Do you think that I talk with people as an excuse of some kind? Do you think that I harbor any illusions about communicating with you? I have no such illusions. The very fact that you have returned here again to talk and discuss shows that you have not heard a thing I am saying. Once that understanding is there, the whole thing is finished for you once and for all. You will not visit any gurus, read any books on this, or listen to anybody. You will not stupidly repeat what others have said, especially what the holy men, saints, and saviors have said. All that is washed out of the system and you are left incapable of following or listening to anyone, not even a God walking the face of the earth, or even a million gods rolled into one. What good is it, after all, when somebody has a billion dollars and you are wondering where your next meal will come from? Anyway, that's not the point. The important thing is: what do you *want*? Please let us forget about your *bhagavans*. Don't sit here and repeat what you have heard from your gurus, it is useless. When once you place your hope, belief, and confidence in your guru, you are stuck with him.

Q: Virtually all the gurus, at least the Eastern ones, have stressed the necessity of being free from one's conditioning, one's past.

U.G.: The past will always be there as long as you want something. Even if you attempt to suppress your wants, the past has to come to your help and tell you HOW to suppress your wants. There is no such differentiation of wants; they are all exactly the same. In the Indian culture the spiritual wants are extolled and sought after, while in the West the material wants prevail.

When wanting ceases, even for a moment, thought is absent and you are left with the simple matter of taking care of the bodily wants -- food, clothes and shelter. To practice some sort of twisted self-denial in which you fail to see to the body's actual physical needs is a silly, perverted way of living.

Q: But the key question remains: how is one not to want?

U.G.: Again you ask "how", thus avoiding the issue. There is no "how" at all. "How" is the trickiest question, for in asking it you are doomed. "How to live?" That is one question that has been bothering people for centuries. Religions claim to give a satisfactory answer to this question. Every teacher claims he knows how. He will be pleased to show you how, for a fee of course. "How to live one's life?" That is the one question which has transformed itself into millions of questions. That is all.

Q: Brushing aside the question of how to be free from constant wanting, it seems obvious from what you have said that one must be free first from the influence of the past, or one's memory. Is this not so?

U.G.: If you go on trying to suppress the past, trying to live in what you call "the present", you will drive yourself crazy. You are trying to control something over which you have no control. It is just not possible to control thought without becoming neurotic, for it is not just your personal, petty little past that is in the way, but the entire past of mankind, the entire memory of every human being, every form of life, and every form of existence. It is not such a simple, easy thing to do. If you try to control the natural flow of the river through all these artificial means--building a dam so to speak--you will inundate and destroy the whole thing. That is why you find thoughts welling up inside you despite your efforts to control, observe, and be aware of them. Once this is understood, then you are never concerned whether thoughts are there or not. When there is an actual need for thought to function, it is there; when there is no need for thought to function, it is not there. You don't even know, and have no way of finding out, whether you are thinking or not. Your *constant* utilization of thought to give continuity to your separative self *is you*. There is nothing there inside you other than that. What you call the "you" is nothing other than the continuity of thought. If that artificial continuity is not there, neither are you. The "you" wants only to function on a different, "higher" level, and not to come to an end. You want to be transformed, to become something else, while continuing. The only way the self can do that is to add more and more experiences to those it has already accumulated.

Q: How does this process of accumulation work?

U.G.: The *only* way the self can add more and more knowledge and experience is to endlessly ask itself the meaningless question "How? How am I to live?" If someone tells you that the continuity of knowledge and experience must come to an end, you ask, "How?", and are right back in the same trap. You are merely asking for the same kind of knowledge.

Q: But we just want to know about enlightenment, if is possible ...

U.G.: You want to know whether there is enlightenment or not, who has it, and how to get it. You are curious about how a supposedly enlightened man would behave, what is the nature of his behavior patterns, and so on. Apparently you know a great deal about enlightenment You must, for you are searching for it.

Q: Not all of us are so naive as to think we can directly search for God, enlightenment, or *nirvana*. So we can accept the illusory nature of such goals. But we are searching for more practical, tangible things like...

MEANING

U.G.: People are looking for enlightenment. You say you are not, but it is the same. Whether you want a new car or simple peace of mind, it is still a painful search. The secular leaders tell you one way, the holy men another way. It makes no difference: as long as you are searching for peace of mind, you will have a tormented mind. If you try not to search, or if you continue to search, you will remain the same. You have to *stop*. You don't stop searching because such an act would be the end of you.

You are lost in a jungle, and you have no way of finding your way out. Night is fast approaching, the wild animals are there, including the cobras, and still you are lost. What do you do in such a situation? You just stop. You don't move...

Q: But we can never be absolutely sure that there is not *some* way out, no matter how fantastic or improbable it may be ...

U.G.: As long as there is that hope that you can somehow or the other get out of the jungle, so long will you continue what you are doing--searching--and so long you feel lost. You are lost only because you are searching. You have no way of finding your way out of the jungle.

Q: So if one could just *stop*...

U.G.: No, that's not it at all. You still expect something to happen. That expectation is part of the problem. That is why you are pursuing these questions. Your expectations are part of your desire to change everything. Nothing needs changing; you must accept life as it is. Through "change" you hope and expect to be born again. What the hell for? This life is enough. There is no peace in this life, no lack of unhappiness, so you wait until your next life to be happy. It's not worth it. You may very well *not* be born again. After all, it is only a hopeful theory to you. You may as well find out for yourself if it is possible to be at peace with yourself *now*.

Q: But all our aspirations, whether material or spiritual, seem to be defined and cast in the mold of our societies, which are, like each of us, corrupt. Yet I must live and struggle within the limits my society has erected around me. My life is not determined solely by my personal aims and attributes, but by what my society allows me to do, that is, by what actual opportunities are made available.

U.G.: You want so many things, and I am not in a position to help you get any of them. You are not clear what you really want. When that which you want is fully recognized, then you must find out how to get what you want. And either you get it or you don't, that's all. So don't bother separating your goals into the low and the lofty. You have been doing that all your life and have not succeeded.

Q: Not just I, but everyone I know seems caught in this trap of endless searching and struggle. We need, do we not, to sit down together and communicate with each other on this ...?

U.G.: As I said, I have no illusions about communication. You cannot share or communicate your experiences with anybody, because, the way you are now functioning, each individual lives in separate and different worlds without any common reference point, and only imagines that you ever communicate with another. It is just not possible.

I cannot communicate and you cannot understand because you have no reference point in regard to what I am saying. When once you have understood that there is nothing to understand, what is there to communicate? Communication is just not necessary. So there is no point in discussing the possibility of communication. Your desire to communicate is part of your general strategy of achievement. Veiled behind that desire for communication is the dependency upon some outside power to solve your problems for you. Except for the quite natural need for practical communication necessary to function in this world, your interest in communication is really an expression of your feelings of helplessness and your hope for the support of some outside agency. Your helplessness persists because of your dependency upon some outside agency. When that dependency upon some outside agency, fictitious or not, is not there, then the feelings of helplessness and the desire to communicate in the abstract, are not there. If the one goes, the other must go also. Your situation and prospects only seem hopeless because you have ideas of hope. Knock off that hope and the crippling feelings of helplessness go with it. There is bound to be helplessness and overwhelming frustration as long as you exist in relationship with the hope for fulfillment, because there is no fulfillment at all. This is the source of your dilemma.

Q: All this is just too much to comprehend and act upon immediately. Perhaps at some time in the future, when I am more able...

U.G.: The future is created by hope, that is the only future that exists. The hope of achieving your goal, the hope of attaining enlightenment, the hope of somehow getting off the merry-go-round -- that is the future. The point from which you project yourself into the future appears to you to be the present, the now. But this is mistaken. There is only the past in operation, and that movement creates the illusion of present and future. You may find what I am saying here logical, or illogical, and you may accept or reject it. But it will in any case be the past that is doing so, for that is all that is in operation within you. It is the past that has projected these goals--God, enlightenment, peace of mind, whatever--and has placed them in the future, out of reach. So happiness is always in the future, tomorrow. A happy man wouldn't be interested in seeking happiness. A well-fed man is not in search of food.

Q: Surely real understanding, of which we are all more or less capable, takes place not in the future, but now, in the present.

U.G.: There is only the past. You have been told by holy men who talk of enlightenment and such nonsense that the past has got to come to a stop before you are free to operate in the "present" and so realize your potential or future possibilities. This I deny.

First of all, why should you be interested in attempting to stop the past from interfering with the present? Be very clear that this idea that the past must die, that time must have an end, has been put into you by those self-appointed guardians of your so-called soul -- the priests, holy men, and saviors of mankind. It is not yours at all. You need to be very clear also about the implications of ending the influence of the past. It is really a dangerous, calamitous thing. In your search to find the end of time, the past, you must use the past. So you only succeed in perpetuating the past. This is a fact, like it or not. Anything you do--having kinder thoughts, behaving selflessly, approaching life negatively rather than positively, listening to holy men, listening to me -- is only adding momentum to the past. All the techniques and methods of achievement at your disposal are from the past, and, therefore, useless. Luckily, there is absolutely nothing to be achieved.

Q: Yes, but I think most of us realize that real happiness is a by-product of something else, and cannot be achieved in and of itself.

U.G.: Your actual approach to happiness is grounded in self-interest and naivete. You are a pleasure seeker at all times, and therefore your ideal of the greatest happiness is simply one of endless pleasure without any pain. When you perceive, if you do at all, the absurdity of such an approach, you then say, "If I could find God and enlightenment I would be free from the contradictory desire to have the one (pleasure) without the other (pain)." So this then becomes your goal, which will take more time to achieve. You are back where you started.

To demand the cessation of the continuity of the movement of the past is ridiculous and unfounded. We have been brainwashed by all these people that if we free ourselves from the past in this life, everything will be hunky-dory, full of lightness and sweetness. It is all romantic hogwash, sheer unadulterated fantasy, and nothing more. You have fallen for this stuff, unfortunately. After all, what is it that you can do? All your actions are from the past. And anything you do only strengthens the hold of pleasure and pain upon you. Ultimately it is all pain and no pleasure. I can say that with certainty, but you are still cock-sure that there is a timeless state, a way out. It is therefore impossible for us to communicate. What I am saying will, if really listened to, put an end to you as you know and experience yourself. You are not listening to me at all. Your so-called listening is all in the past. The constant interpretation by the past of what is being said prevents you from listening to what is being said.

All I can guarantee you is that as long as you are searching for happiness, you will remain unhappy. This is a fact. Society is so organized and complex that you have no other way of surviving except to accept the way of life around you as organized, along with the limitations it places upon all of us. We must all accept the reality of society, whether we like it or not. But this is not what we are talking about. What we are talking about is altogether different. All your relationships, knowledge, and experiences, all your emotions and feelings, all that romantic stuff, belongs entirely to society, not to you. You are not an individual at all; you are secondhand people.

Only when you are free from what every man and woman has thought and felt before you will you become an individual. Such an individual will not go around attempting to destroy everything that belongs to society. He is not in conflict with society at all. He would never tear down the temples and institutions or burn books that men have made with great care. He would not be a rebel. All the accumulated knowledge, experience, and suffering of mankind is inside of you. You must build a huge bonfire within you. Then you will become an individual. There is no other way. Society is built on a foundation of conflict, and *you are society*. Therefore you*must* always be in conflict with society. The real individual, one who is free of the accumulated tradition and knowledge of mankind, is necessarily a threat to that society. Society, of which you are a part, cannot be other than it is. So stop trying to save it or change it. You cannot even change your mother-in-law.

Q: Not all of us are so obsessed with our own personal happiness and salvation. Many of us are socially, politically aware, and merely wish to create a new world, a differently organized society, so that poverty, injustice, and other social wrongs are corrected. You talk as if we all were fixated on only our own personal problems and goals, while in fact most of us want to be of service to the world and seek not selfish ends, but simply a better, more humane society.

U.G.: You want to change yourself into something and at the same time find you cannot change at all. This "change" you talk of is really just more romantic fancy stuff for you. You never change, only think about changing. As long as you want to change, for some reason or the other, so long will you insist upon changing the whole world. You want a different world so that you can be happy in it. That is your only interest. You can talk of mankind, concern for mankind, compassion for mankind, but it is all bullshit, horseshit ...

Since you are determined to bring about change -- a notion put into you by your culture -- you remain discontent and want the world to be different. When your inner demand to be something different from what in fact you are comes to an end, then the neurotic demand to change your society ceases. Then you cannot be in conflict with society. You are in perfect harmony with society, including its brutalities and miseries. All your attempts to change this brutal society only add momentum to it. This is not to say that the free individual is indifferent to society. On the contrary. In any case, it is you who are indifferent right now. You only talk and whine, meanwhile doing nothing. Sorry...

Q: But it is very urgent that we have peace in the world.

U.G.: Unless you are at peace with yourself, there cannot be peace around the world. When are you going to be at peace yourself? Next life? No chance. Wait, you will see. Even then there is no guarantee that your society will be peaceful. They will not be at peace. When you are at peace with yourself, that is the end of the story.

Q: It seems that we have only this *idea* of a peaceful society, while actually our relationship to others is quite violent. How do we bridge this gap between the ideal and the actual?

U.G.: You are trying to establish relationships with people around you, with society, with the whole world. For some reason or other the actual relationships are very ugly and horrible. Have you noticed that as long as our relationships satisfy the question, "What can I get out of this relationship?", as long as they can be directed to serve my personal happiness, there is no conflict? Every person is in the same situation: his relationships are harmonious as long as they serve his own ideas of happiness. And we also demand that our happiness be permanent. In the very nature of things this is impossible. There is no such thing as permanence at all. Everything is constantly changing. Everything is in flux. Because you cannot face the impermanence of all relationships, you invent sentiments, romance, and dramatic emotions to give them continuity. Therefore you are always in conflict.

Q: So perhaps we should abandon the search for perfect, harmonious relationships and concentrate on understanding ourselves -- is that it?

U.G.: Understanding yourself is one of the greatest jokes, perpetrated on the gullible and credulous people everywhere, not only by the purveyors of ancient wisdom--the holy men--but also by the modern scientists. The psychologists love to talk about self-knowledge, self-actualization, living from moment to moment, and such rot. These absurd ideas are thrown at us as if they are something new.

Q: This must be boring for you, responding to the same old questions wherever you go.

U.G.: I have been everywhere in the world, meeting and talking with people. People are exactly the same the world over. The questions never vary. But I am never bored with it. How can I be bored? If I were some sort of fool getting some sort of kick out of this, looking for new, better and different questions, then there would be a possibility of getting bored. But I am not looking for anything So boredom is impossible. Are you bored? You have no way of finding out for yourself.

Q: I am bored because I am average, like everyone else. It is my mediocrity that makes life seem so empty and boring ...

U.G.: It is very difficult to be like the other fellow, to be ordinary. Mediocrity takes a great deal of energy. But to be ourselves is very easy. You don't have to do a thing. No effort is necessary. You don't have to exercise your will. You need not do a thing to be yourself. But to be something other than what you are, you have to do a lot of things. The boredom and restlessness you feel inside you is there only because you think you must be doing something more interesting, more meaningful, and more valuable than what you are already doing. You think that the way you are carrying on is terrible boring, and that there *must* be something more valuable, powerful, and exciting to do. So all this becomes part of the complex knowledge you have about yourself. The more you know about yourself the more impossible it becomes to be humble and sensitive. How can there be humility as long as you know something?

Q: There is something in me that finds it difficult to be simple about all this. There seems to be a fear of...

U.G.: All fears lead eventually to the fear of death, physical death. You are attempting to push the fear of death way into the

MEANING

background so you can continue, that is all. As long as you are fear-ridden, there can be no sense in discussing the meaning of life. Why ask questions and mystify life? You are alive because your parents had sex, period. Don't look for a meaning to life. There may not be any meaning at all. It may have its own meaning that you can never know. Obviously life has no meaning for you. Otherwise you would not be here asking these questions. Everything you do seems absolutely meaningless, that is the fact, Don't bother about others. The whole world is an extension of you. The way you are thinking, feeling, and experiencing is exactly the same way everyone else in this world is thinking, feeling, and experiencing. The goal may be different, but the mechanism and instrument you are using to achieve your particular goal is not a whit different from that used by others to achieve theirs. Why should there be any meaning in living? The moment a baby arrives in the world it is interested in one thing: survival. The instinct in the baby to feed itself, to survive, and to reproduce itself seems to be the way of life. It is life expressing itself. That is all. You needn't impose a meaning upon it.

Q: Living itself does not seem to be enough. We have aspirations and goals, and we feel that there must be a more sane and meaningful way of living.

U.G.: Instead of living, you are obsessed with the question, "How am I to live?" That dilemma is put into us by our culture, and is the one responsible for many of our problems. Because you are dead, not living what we call life, you are concerned with HOW to live. If you succeed in getting rid of the idea of somehow living a better, nobler, and more meaningful life, you will replace that belief with another. You must face the fact that you know nothing about life or the living of it.

Q: In spite of the fact that we are not living, we are terrified of death.

U.G.: The body responds to life around it: the pulse of the heart, the various physiological processes, the throb of life all indicate the presence of life. When these processes stop, then what you call clinical death takes place. Next we observe the body breaking down into its constituent elements, in turn assuming new and different life forms. But this continuity of life in new forms is little consolation to you, for you want to continue in your present form, warts and all. If you bury the body, the worms have a field day. If you throw it into the water, the fish will have a feast. That life will continue no matter what. But you will not be there to experience death. There is only death in the clinical sense.

Q: If I am not really living, if I cannot know death, if I really don't give a damn about society, if my life is actually meaningless, if my hard-won self-knowledge is just an expression of ignorance, then what I take to be reality is a projection of my own mind ...

U.G.: Where is this mind you talk of? Can you show it to me? There is no such thing as your mind and my mind. Mind is everywhere, sort of like the air we breathe. There is a thought sphere. It is not ours and not mine. It is always there. Your brain acts like an antenna, picking and choosing what signals it wants to

MEANING

use. That is all. You use the signals for purposes of communication.

First of all, we have to communicate with ourselves. We begin as children naming everything over and over again. Communicating with others is a little more complex and comes next. The problem, or the pathology if you will, arises when you constantly communicate with yourself, irrespective of any outside demand for thought. You are all the time communicating with yourself: "I am happy...I am not happy...What is the meaning of life?..." and so on. If that incessant communication within yourself is not there, *you* are not there as you now know and experience yourself. When that inner monologue is no longer there, the need to communicate with others is absent. So you communicate with others only to maintain that communication you are having with yourself, your inner monologue. This kind of communication is possible only when you rely and draw upon the vast totality of thoughts passed on by man from generation to generation. Man has through the process of evolution learned to draw from this storehouse quicker, subtler, and more refined thoughts than the rest of the animals. They have powerful instincts. Through thinking man has enabled himself to survive more efficiently than the other species. This ability of thought to adapt is the curse of man.

Q: Whether you lay it at the door of society, the genes, evolution or the influence of the stars, it comes down to the same thing: we are all deeply conditioned and need to be free of that conditioning in order to function naturally and freely. This is obvious, isn't it?

U.G.: It is not at all obvious to me. It is just not possible for you to be without conditioning. No matter what you do, you are conditioned. The "unconditioning" that the spiritual gurus are talking about is a bogus affair. The notion of being unconditioned, of unconditioning oneself, is just another item for sale in the marketplace of the holy business. It has no validity. You will find out. Anything you do is conditioned. Unconditioning yourself has no meaning. What you have to be free from is the very desire to be free from conditioning. Conditioning is intelligence, the ability to respond adequately to the environment. This is entirely unrelated to your fantasies, ideations, and mentations, what you take to be the heights of intelligence.

Q: If inquiry, self-knowledge, and unconditioning don't help to solve my basic dilemma, then perhaps science can help through life-extension techniques or genetic engineering...

U.G.: Even genetic engineering that the scientists are indulging in is not for the benefit of mankind. If they succeed, it will be handed over to the state. The state will use it to control everything and everyone. Brainwashing, which takes centuries, would be obsolete. Through a simple injection of genetically engineered substances into the body, the state can turn its citizens into bloodthirsty soldiers, mindless bureaucrats, or whatever type it wants.

Q: Perhaps we are complicating it. Could it be that we are all just too shallow in thought, that we only lack sufficient vision and mental scope?

U.G.: Forget it. In any event your actions must be destructive of man's ultimate interests, for they are born out of thought, which is a dead thing. Forcing life to fit your dead ideas and assumptions is your basic difficulty. Everything you stand for, believe in, experience, and aspire to is the result of thought. And thought is destructive because it is nothing more than a protective mechanism, programmed to protect its own interests at all costs. Anyhow, are there really thoughts? Are you thinking now? You have no way of knowing.

Q: But it is a superhuman task to fully understand though, is it not? All religions and important philosophies have put before us a more or less superhuman figure who has somehow transcended the relative world--the world of thought if you will--and attained great heights. But we are ordinary men not capable of colossal, fearless, or intrepid actions.

U.G.: If you are freed from the goal of the `perfect`, `godly`, or `truly religious` supermen, then that which is natural in man begins to express itself. Your religious and secular culture has placed before you the ideal man or woman, the perfect human being, and then tries to fit everybody into that mold. It is impossible. Nature is busy creating absolutely unique individuals, whereas culture has invited a single mold to which all must conform. It is grotesque.

Q: So you are not a perfect man as some claim?

U.G.: I wish I knew, but I don't want to bother. Who cares? I have no way of finding out, and if I did, it would be a tragedy for the world. They would make of me a model and attempt to live a certain way, creating a disaster for mankind. We have enough gurus, why add one more?

Q: If you are not a teacher, a guru of some sort, then why do you talk to us? It appears to us that you are giving some kind of instruction, that you are expressing a teaching that can be of use to mankind.

U.G.: I am just singing my song, then I go. If someone listens to me or not, it is not my concern. I don't consider any hypothetical situation. If nobody comes and talks, it is all right with me. Believe me, my talking is only incidental, it is not aimed at liberating anyone. I've been coming to this area for thirty years. If you are not here, maybe I'll watch the TV, or read crime fiction -- it's all the same for me. I am not selling anything. This is so. I am simply pointing out that at the rate at which we are going the whole genetic engineering technology will end up in the hands of the political system to be used for the complete control and subjugation of man.

Q: If this danger is really so imminent, then it is urgent that others "stumble" into their natural state, as you indicate happened to you, if for no other reason than to prove the existence of an alternative to genetic totalitarianism. Would you go along with this?

U.G.: No. This natural state cannot be used to further anyone's crusade. Nor am I interested in setting myself up as an archetype or prophet for mankind. I am not interested in satisfying the curiosity of anybody. The scientists are making tremendous progress in the fields of microbiology and glandular and brain physiology. They will soon have enough sophistication in these areas to understand the physiological mutation that took place within me. I personally cannot make any definite statement except to say that the whole mechanism is an automatic thing. The interference of thought is not there anymore. Thought is functional in value, nothing more. It operates temporarily here when there is a demand from the environment, but cannot act with regard to becoming something or to changing things there. This is all. That is *energy*, an energy that can make functioning in this world sanely and intelligently an easy affair. Now you are wasting that energy by attempting to be something other than what you in fact are. Then you will have a certainty which cannot be transmitted by me or by anybody.

I have discovered for myself and by myself, that what we have been told about freedom, enlightenment, and God is false. No power in the world can touch this. This does not make me superior. Nothing of the sort. To feel superior or inferior you must separate yourself from the world. I do not look upon the world as a separate thing as you do. The knowledge I have bout the world--whether within or without--comes into operation only when there is a demand for it. Otherwise I simply don't know. Your natural state is one of not knowing.

Q: You make no special claims for yourself. Yet your listeners, including myself, sense a certainty and authority in what you say. Does not this indicate that you are in fact a free man?

U.G.: The knowledge that you are this, that you are that, that you are happy, that you are unhappy, that you are a realized man, that you are not a realized man, is completely absent here. You, or I, have no way of knowing if we are free men. Nothing tells me that I am a free man. In your case the naming process, the wanting something, the questioning goes on and on no matter what. Here thought functions only from a stimulus from the outside. Even then the response of knowledge is instantaneous, and I am back again like a big question mark. Your constant demand to experience the same thing over and over again results in compulsive, repetitive thinking. I don't see any need or reason for the repetitive process to go on and on. In my case there is no one separate from this functioning, no one who can step back and say, "This is reality." There is no such thing as reality at all. Reality is imposed upon us by culture, society, and education. Don't get me wrong. Thought has a functional value. If we don't accept the world as it is imposed on us, we will end up in the loony bin. I have to accept it as a relative fact. Otherwise there is no way of experiencing the reality of anything. It is thought that has created the reality of your body, of your living, of your sleep, and of all your perceptions. You experience this reality through knowledge. Otherwise there is no way of your knowing for yourself that you have a body, that you are alive, that you are awake. All that is knowledge. The reality of anything is something which cannot be experienced by anybody.

Q: We have found this talk most interesting. Thank you very much.

5

SILENCE

Q: U.G., I have read a statement that is attributed to you. It says that nature is not interested in creating a perfect being, but that its interest is only to create a perfect species. What do you mean by that?

U.G.: We have for centuries been made to believe that the end product of human evolution, if there is one, is the creation of perfect beings modeled after the great spiritual teachers of mankind and their behavior patterns.

Q: By great spiritual teachers you mean people like Jesus and the Buddha?

U.G.: All of them. All the great teachers - the occidental, the oriental, and the Chinese teachers. That is the basic problem we are confronted with. I don't think I have any special insights into the laws of nature. But if there is any such thing as an end product of human evolution (I don't know if there is such a thing as evolution, but we take it for granted that there is), what nature is trying to produce is not a perfect being.

Q: But scientific research has revealed that there is such a thing as evolution.

U.G.: Even today some universities don't allow their students to study Darwin's Origin of Species. His statements have been proved to be wrong to some extent because he said that acquired characteristics cannot be transmitted to the succeeding generations. But every time they [the scientists] discover something new they change their theories.

Nature does not use anything as a model. It is only interested in perfecting the species. It is trying to create perfect species and not perfect beings. We are not ready to accept that. What nature has created in the form of human species is something extraordinary. It is an unparalleled creation. But culture is interested in fitting the actions of all human beings into a common mold. That is because it is interested in maintaining the status quo, its value system. That is where the real conflict is. This [referring to himself] is something which cannot be fitted into that value system.

Q: I have been in touch with your statements over the years. You can be called a universal pessimist. Given your position, I

am tempted to ask, "Why don't you commit suicide?" I cannot deny that you are also a very lively person.

U.G.: Since I have not come into the world of my own choice, I don't think I will opt for suicide. It is not a clever statement that I am making, but these labels that I am a pessimist and others are optimists do not really mean anything. They have put me into the framework of a pessimist, a nihilist, an atheist, and many others. How can you, for instance, call me a god man when I sometimes go to the extent of saying that God is irrelevant? If I make a statement like that, I don't mean that I am questioning the existence of God. I am not impressed by the theologians discussing everlastingly, trying to impress upon us through their dialectical thinking, the cosmological, ontological, and teleological proofs for the existence of God. We are not concerned with that question at all. It has become irrelevant to us because we use that to exploit others. We use thinking as an instrument of destruction. We want to believe that God is on our side. During the last world war, the Germans claimed that God was their copilot, and the British also claimed that God was their copilot. Both of them destroyed life and property. So we would like God to be on our side all the time and use Him. But what has come out of that is only violence. Belief in God, or belief in anything, separates us from others. When we find that we cannot force our beliefs on others we resort to violence. We would like everybody to believe the same thing. When we fail in that attempt of ours to make everybody believe in God, or no God, or even our political systems - the right or the left -, what is left is only violence.

Q: I began with this whole question of nature because what I find in your statements is a profound sense of nature, a profound sense of the absolute and primitive reality of life itself, which seems to me an extraordinarily positive force and a force for the good.

U.G.: The fundamental mistake that humanity made somewhere along the line, is, or was, or whatever is the correct verb [*chuckles*], to experience this separateness from the totality of life. At that time there occurred in man, which includes woman also, this self-consciousness which separated him from the life around. He was so isolated that it frightened him. The demand to be part of the totality of life around him created this tremendous demand for the ultimate. He thought that the spiritual goals of God, truth, or reality, would help him to become part of the 'whole' again. But the very attempt on his part to become one with or become integrated with the totality of life has kept him only more separate. Isolated functioning is not part of nature. But this isolation has created a demand for finding out ways and means of becoming a part of nature. But thought in its very nature can only create problems and cannot help us solve them.

We don't seem to realize that it is thought that is separating us from the totality of things. The belief that this is the one that can help us to keep in tune with the totality is not going to materialize. So, it has come up with all kinds of ingenuous, if I may use that word, ideas of insight and intuition.

Q: There are a lot of words.

U.G.: Yes, we have a plethora of words. You know it is said that Shakespeare, that great playwright and poet, had a vocabulary of only four thousand words. I don't know if that is true. But now we have many thousands of words. We come up with every kind of phrase to cover up this impossibility of trying to use words to understand the reality of things. That is where the real problem is. Thought has not succeeded so far in understanding reality, but that [thought] is all that we are left with. We cannot question thought. We cannot brush it aside. We know in a way that it cannot help us, but can only create problems. We are not ready to throw it out and find out if there is any other way, if there is any answer.

Q: **One of the things that strike me as you speak is how in many ways what you say is related to the underlying philosophy of Hinduism. I mean Hinduism that speaks of the original unity of all things.**

U.G.: I am not for a moment expounding Hinduism here or in India. In fact, they think that I am not a Hindu. Yet the Hindus are ready to accept [to some degree] what I am saying. They say, "What you are saying seems to be true, but the way you are putting things is not acceptable". They brush me aside. But at the same time they cannot totally brush me aside. They always try to fit me into their framework or reference point. If they cannot do that, the whole tradition in which they have a tremendous investment is at stake. So they necessarily have to try to fit me into that framework. So far nobody has succeeded. Many philosophers in India have been asked about my statements, and they know that they can very well deal with any philosophy, any thinker, past and present, but they have some difficulty in fitting me into any particular frame that they know of. What they say is, and I quote, "There is no way we can fit this man into any known cage. So what we have to do is to let the bird fly."

Q: I suppose that the 'free flying' fits in perfectly with primitive nature.

U.G.: You know what the word 'religion' means?

Q: It is to be tied down in some way.

U.G.: I am not interested in the root meaning of the words at all, but it means "to connect you back to the source."

Q: Yes.

U.G.: On the other hand, religion has created schisms. It has been responsible for tremendous destruction of life and property. It is very unfortunate. But, nevertheless, the fact does remain that religion has failed in its purpose.

We live in the hope and die in the hope that somehow the very same thing that has failed us will one day rescue us. You cannot conceive of the impossibility of creating a harmony between humans and the life around through thought.

Q: Although religion has no doubt done many destructive things, it has also done many creative things. I mean great art and literature. Shakespeare himself, in a way, was coming out of basically a religious experience. Certainly that is true of the

Western civilization, which arises out of the Christian experience.

U.G.: That's true. That is why when a void is created, when all the systems have failed, there is the danger of a demand for the religious stuff stepping into it and trying to tell us, "We have the answers for your problems." But the revolutions have failed. I am not against any value system, but the demand to fit ourselves into it [a value system] is the cause of man's suffering.

Q: Where then do we go from here? I am not going to ask you what is the purpose of life, because obviously, as you were saying, that is really not a relevant question.

U.G.: No. It is a relevant question, but is born out of the assumption that we know about life. Nobody knows anything about life. We have only concepts, ideations, and mentations about life. Even the scientists who are trying to understand life and its origin come up only with theories and definitions of life. You may not agree with me, but all thought, all thinking is dead. Thinking is born out of dead ideas. Thought or the thinking mechanism trying to touch life, experience it, capture, and give expression to it are impossible tasks.

What we are concerned about is living. Living is our relationship with our fellow beings, with the life around. When we have everything that we can reasonably ask for, all the material comforts that you have in the West, the question naturally arises: "Is that all?" The moment you pose that question to yourself, we have created a problem. If that's all there is, what then is the next step to take? We do not see any meaning in our life, and so we pose this question to ourselves, and throw this question at all those who you think have answers.

What is the meaning of life? What is the purpose of life? It may have its own meaning, it may have its own purpose. By understanding the meaning of life and the purpose of life we are not going to improve, change, modify, or alter our behavior patterns in any way. But there is a hope that by understanding the meaning of life, we can bring about a change. There may not be any meaning of life. If it has a meaning, it is already in operation there. Wanting to understand the meaning of life seems to be a futile attempt on our part. We go on asking these questions.

Once a very old gentleman, ninety-five years old, who was considered to be a great spiritual man and who taught the great scriptures all the time to his followers, came to see me. He heard that I was there in that town. He came to me and asked me two questions. He asked me, "What is the meaning of life? I have written hundreds of books telling people all about the meaning and purpose of life, quoting all the scriptures and interpreting them. I haven't understood the meaning of life. You are the one who can give an answer to me." I told him, "Look, you are ninety-five years old and you haven't understood the meaning of life. When are you going to understand the meaning of life? There may not be any meaning to life at all." The next question he asked me was, "I have lived ninety-five years and I am going to die one of these days. I want to know what will happen after my death." I said, "You may not live long to know anything about death. You have to die now. Are you ready to die?" As long as you are asking the question, "What is death?" or "What is there after death?" you are already dead. These are all dead questions. A living man would never ask those questions.

Q: Let us ask then another question which is not intellectual. What should we do?

U.G.: [*Laughs*] We have been for centuries told what to do. Why are we asking the same question, "What to do?" What to do in relation to what? What I am emphasizing is that the demand to bring about a change in ourselves is the cause of our suffering. I may say that there is nothing to be changed. But the revolutionary teachers come and tell us that there is something there in which you have to bring about a radical revolution. Then we assume there is such a thing as soul, spirit, or the 'I'. What I assert all the time is that I haven't found anything like the self or soul there.

This question haunted me all my life, and suddenly it hit me: "There is no self to realize. What the hell have I been doing all this time?" You see, that hits you like a lightning. Once that hits you, the whole mechanism of the body that is controlled by this thought [of the 'I'] is shattered. What is left is the tremendous living organism with an intelligence of its own. What you are left with is the pulse, the beat, and the throb of life.

"There must be something more, and we have to do something to become part of the whole thing." Such demands have arisen because of our assumption that we have been created for a grander purpose than that for which other species on this planet have been created. That's the fundamental mistake we have made. Culture is responsible for our assuming this. We thus come to believe that the whole creation is for the benefit of man. The demand to use nature for our purposes has created all the ecological problems. It is not such an easy thing for us to deal with these problems. We have reached a point where there is no going back. You may say that I am a pessimist again.

The point is, we have probably arrived at a place where there is no going back. What is the fate of mankind and what is one to do? Anything that is born out of thought is destructive in its nature. That is why I very often say in my conversations and interviews that thought, in its birth, in its nature, in its expression, and in its action, is fascist. Thought is interested in protecting itself, and is always creating frontiers around itself. And it wants to protect the frontiers. That is why we create frontiers around us: our families, our nations, and then this planet. I am talking all the time. What is your third question ? [*Laughter*]

Q: I am fascinated because this is one of the most consistently intellectual conversations I have had in a long time.

U.G.: [*Laughs*] Whatever else I may or may not have been, I have never been an intellectual. People ask me questions, and I say that I am an illiterate.

Q: Well, your logic is absolutely consistent. The consistency of your position is unassailable. It would seem to me that the best thing to do in some way is what some of the Christian mystics did. They said that God is nothing.

U.G.: Remarkable people.

Q: That leads them to a silence almost to the end. Why do you speak? I pose the question to you.

U.G.: Why do I speak?

Q: Yes.

U.G.: Why do I speak? [Laughter] Am I speaking? You know, it may sound very funny to you. I have nothing to say, and what I am saying is not born out of my thinking. You may not accept this. But it is not a logically ascertained premise that I am putting across. It may sound very funny to you, and you have put me in a very precarious position by asking me why I am talking. Am I talking? Really I am not, you see. There is nobody who is talking here. I use this simile of a ventriloquist. He is actually carrying on both sides of the dialogue, but we attribute one side of it to the dummy in front of him. In exactly the same way, all your questions are born out of the answers you already have. Any answer anybody gives should put an end to your questions. But it does not. And we are not ready to accept the fact that all the questions are born out of the answers. If the questions go, the answers we take for granted also go with them. But we are not ready to throw the answers away, because sentiment comes into the picture. The tremendous investment we have made, and the faith we have in the teachers, are also at stake. Therefore, we are not ready to brush aside the answers.

Actually we do not want answers for our questions. The assumption that the questions are different from the questioner is also false. If the answer goes, the questioner also goes. The questioner is nothing but the answers. That is really the problem. We are not ready to accept this answer because it will put an end to the answers which we have accepted for ages as the real answers.

Q: And so, we keep asking questions.

U.G.: Yes, asking questions.

Q: And where would we have been without a few questions to ask? [*Laughter*]

U.G.: You have asked the questions and I have tried to give the answers.

Q: Do you say that we are two separate people or just part of the universal life force?

U.G.: There is no way I can separate myself except when I use the knowledge which is common to us both. So there is no way I can create this individual here [pointing to himself] and experience that there is such a thing as a human body here, that there is something that is talking here. There is nobody who is talking. It is just a computer. And, you are interested in operating the computer. Whatever is coming out of me that you think is the answer is a printout.

What I am trying to say is that I have no image of myself. I have no way I can create the image. The only instruments I have are my sensory perceptions. My sensory perceptions function independently of each other. There is no coordinator who is coordinating all the sensory perceptions and creating an image.

Since I have no way I can create an image here within me, I have no way of creating an image of you and put you up there. But it does not mean that I am this microphone, or you, or that table. It is not that I am the table, or the microphone, or this glass of water, or this visitors' card; not at all. There is no way, however, that I can separate myself from any of these except through the help of the knowledge which is our common property. The questions get answered through that knowledge. That is also the only way I can experience things.

Actually what we see here [in ourselves] is the opposite of what we would like to be, what we would want to be, what we think ought to be or should be. Otherwise there is no way you can create an image of yourself. Since you want to be something other than what you are, (that's what the culture has put in there,) you create something which is the opposite [of what you would like to be]. That is all the time struggling to be something other than what it is. So what is here is the opposite of what you would like to be, and so that creates time. Thought can never conceive the possibility of achieving anything except in time. It does not want to let go of this image which is created by what you would like to be, what you think you ought to be or should be. That's really the problem.

"What is going on here are two persons exchanging ideas" - this I really don't know. I have no way of experiencing that at all. But if you ask me the question, "Who is it that is talking?" I say it is U.G. and you. It may take a little time because the computer has to come up with the information that is there. I mean not in a simple case like this but in more complex cases.

We think that our memory is very fast. But actually it is slower than the activity of the sensory perceptions. There is an illusion that memory is operating all the time, trying to capture everything within its framework. But the illusion is created by the mind in order to maintain the continuity of our identity. We can't afford to let go of our identity whether we are asleep, awake or dreaming. This identity is there all the time, and we do not want to let go of it.

I am not saying that thought is useless or any such thing. Its interest is to maintain its continuity. When the identity is not there, you have no way of identifying yourself with anything except through the help of knowledge. So, I do accept, like anyone else, the reality of the world as it is imposed on me. Otherwise I would end up in the loony-bin, singing loony tunes and merry melodies. But at the same time, I know that thought is merely functional in its nature and it cannot help me become something which I am not.

6

EXTRAORDINARY

There is no teaching of mine and never shall be one. A teaching implies a method or a system, a technique or a new way of thinking to be applied in order to bring about a transformation in your way of life. What I am saying is outside the field of teachability. It is simply a description of the way I am functioning. It is just a description of the natural state of man. This is the way you, stripped of the machinations of thought, are also functioning. The natural state is not the state of a self-realized, God-realized man. It is not a thing to be achieved or attained. It is not a thing to be willed into existence. It is there. It is the living state.

This state is just the functional activity of life. By life I do not mean something abstract but the life of the senses functioning naturally without the interference of thought. Thought is an interloper which thrusts itself into the affairs of the senses. It has a profit motive. Thought directs the activity of the senses to get something out of them and uses them to give continuity to itself.

Your natural state has no relationship whatsoever with the religious states of bliss and ecstasy. They lie within the field of experience. Those who have led man on his search for religiousness throughout the centuries have perhaps experienced those religious states, so can you. They are thought-induced states of being and as they come so do they go. All are trips in the wrong direction. They are all within the field of time. Timeless can never be experienced, grasped, contained, much less given expression to, by any man. That beaten track will lead you nowhere. There is no oasis situated yonder. You are stuck with the mirage.

This state is a physical condition of your being. It is not some kind of psychological mutation. It is not a state of mind into which you can fall one day and out of the next. You can't imagine the extent to which, as you are now, thought pervades and interferes with the functioning of every cell in your body. Coming into your natural state will blast every cell, every gland, every nerve. It is a chemical change. An alchemy of some sort takes place. But this state has nothing to do with the experiences of chemical drugs. Those are experiences, this is not.

Does such a thing as enlightenment exist? To me what does exist is a purely physical process. There is nothing mystical or spiritual about it. If I close the eyes some light penetrates through the eyelids. If I cover the eyelids there is still light inside. There seems to be some kind of a hole in the forehead which doesn't show but through which something penetrates. In India that light is golden, in Europe it is blue.

There is also some kind of light penetration through the back of the head. It's as if there is a hole running through between those spots in front and back of the skull. There is nothing inside but this light. If you cover those points there is complete, total darkness. This light doesn't do anything or help the body to function in any way, it's just there.

This state is a state of not knowing. You really don't know what you are looking at. All there is inside is wonderment. It is a state of wonder because I just do not know what I am looking at. The knowledge about it, all that I have learned, is held in the background unless there is a demand. When required it comes quickly like an arrow, then I am back in the state of not knowing, of wonder.

You can never understand the tremendous peace that is always there within you that is your natural state. Your trying to create a peaceful state of mind is in fact creating disturbance within you. You can only talk of peace, create a state of mind and say to yourself that you are very peaceful, but that is not peace, that is violence. There is no use in practicing peace or reason to cultivate silence. Real silence is explosive. It is not the dead state of mind that spiritual seekers think. That doesn't mean anything at all. This is volcanic in its nature. It's bubbling all the time—the energy, the life—that is its quality.

Life is aware of itself, if we can put it that way. It is conscious of itself. When I talk of feeling I do not mean the same thing that you do. Actually, feeling is a physical response, a thud in the thymus. The thymus, one of the endocrine glands, is located under the breast bone. When you come into your natural state, sensations are felt there. You don't translate them as good or bad. They are just a thud. If there is a movement outside of you in your field of vision, that movement is also felt in the thymus. The whole of your being is that movement, or vibrates with that sound. There is no separation. This does not mean that you identify yourself with it. There is no you there, nor is there any object. What causes that sensation you don't know. You do not even know that it is a sensation.

Affection (this is not my interpretation of the word) means that you are affected by everything, not that some emotion flows from you towards something. The natural state is a state of great sensitivity, but this is a physical sensitivity of the senses, not some kind of emotional compassion or tenderness for others. There is compassion only in the sense that there are no others for me and so there is no separation. Actually, there is always a gap between any two sensations. The coordinator bridges that gap, establishes itself as an illusion of continuity. In the natural state, there is no entity coordinating the messages from the different senses, each sense is functioning independently in its own way.

When there is a demand from outside which makes it necessary to coordinate the senses and come up with a response, still there is no coordinator but there is a temporary state of coordination. There is no continuity. When the demand has been met, again there is only the uncoordinated, disconnected, disjointed functioning of the senses. This is always the case. Once the continuity is blown apart, not that it was ever there but the illusory continuity, it's finished once and for all.

All that you know lies within the framework of your experience, which is of thought. This state is not an experience. I am only trying to give you a feel of it, which is, unfortunately, misleading. When there is no coordinator, there is no linking of sensations, there is no translating of sensations. They stay pure and simple sensations. I do not even know that they are sensations. I may look at you as you are talking. The eyes will focus on your mouth because that is what is moving and the ears will receive the sound vibrations. There is nothing inside which links up the two and says that it is you talking.

What functions is a primordial consciousness untouched by thought. The eyes are like a very sensitive camera. The physiologists say that light reflected off objects strikes the retina of the eye and the sensation goes through the optic nerve to the brain. The faculty of sight, of seeing, is simply a physical phenomenon. It makes no difference to the eyes what they are focused on, they produce sensations in exactly the same way. The eyes look on everyone and everything without discrimination. Left to themselves they do not linger but are moving all the time. They are drawn by the things outside. Movement attracts them, or brightness, or a color which stands out from whatever is around it.

There is no self looking. The consciousness is like a mirror reflecting whatever is there outside. The depth, the distance, the color—everything is there, but there is nobody who is translating these things. Unless there is a demand for knowledge about what I am looking at, there is no separation, no distance from what is there. There is a kind of clarity.

The eyes do not blink except when there is sudden danger. This is something very natural because things outside are demanding attention all the time. Then when the eyes are tired they may be open but the vision is blurred. If they stay open all the time, if the reflex action of blinking is not operating, they become dry and there are some glands beyond the outer corners of the eyes, not activated in your case, which act as a watering mechanism. But by practicing not blinking one will not arrive in this state, one will only strain the eyes. Once you are in your natural state, by some luck or some strange chance, all this happens in its own way.

When I am walking and suddenly see something different because the light has changed, this consciousness suddenly expands to the size of the object in front of the body and the lungs take a deep breath. This is pranayama, not hyperventilation or inhaling through one nostril and exhaling through the other. This pranayama is going on all the time. So there is consciousness of a sudden change in the breathing and then it moves on to something else. It is always moving. It does not linger on something which thought has decided is beautiful. There is no one directing.

As for listening, when you leave the sense of hearing alone all that is there is the vibration of the sound. The words repeat themselves inside of you as in an echo chamber. This sense is functioning in just the same way with you except that you think the words you are hearing come from outside of you.

EXTRAORDINARY

Get this straight—you can never hear one word from anyone no matter how intimately you think you are in relationship with that person. You hear only your own translations always. They are all your words you are hearing. All that the other person's words can possibly be to you is a noise, a vibration picked up by the eardrum and transferred to the nerves which run to the brain. You are translating those vibrations all the time trying to understand because you want to get something out of what you are hearing. When there is no translation, all languages sound the same whether or not your particular knowledge structure speaks a particular language. The only differences are in the spacing of the syllables and in the tune. Languages are melodic in different ways but the appreciation of music, poetry and language is all culturally determined and is the product of thought.

Your movement of thought interferes with the process of touch just as it does with the other senses. Anything you touch is always translated as hard, soft, warm, cold, wet, dry and so on. Without this thought process there is no body consciousness, there are only isolated points of contact, impulses of touch which are not tied together by thought. So the body is not different from the objects around it. It is a set of sensations like any others. Your body does not belong to you.

Perhaps I can give you the feel of this. I sleep for four hours at night no matter what time I go to bed then I lie in bed until morning fully awake. I don't know what is lying there in the bed. I don't know whether I'm lying on my left side or my right side. For hours and hours I lie like this. If there is any noise outside, it just echoes in me. I listen to my heartbeat and don't know what it is.

There are only the sensations of touch from points of contact and the gravitational pull, nothing inside links up these things. Even if the eyes are open and looking at the whole body there are still only the points of contact and they have no connection with what I am looking at. If I want to try to link up these points of contact into the shape of my own body probably I will succeed but by the time it is completed the body is back in the same situation of different points of contact. The linkage cannot stay.

My talking comes out in response to the questions which are asked. I cannot sit and give a talk on the natural state. That is an artificial situation for me. There is nobody who is thinking thoughts and then coming out with answers. This state is expressing itself. I really don't know what I'm saying and what I'm saying is of no importance. You may transcribe my own talking but it will make no sense to me. It is a dead thing.

What is here, this natural state, is a living thing. It cannot be captured by me, let alone by you. It's like a flower. This simile is all I can give. It just blooms. It's there. As long as it is there it has a fragrance which is different and distinct from that of every other flower. You may not recognize it. It's of no importance. You can't preserve its perfume. Whatever you preserve of this is not the living thing. Preserving the expressions, teachings or words of such a man has no meaning. This state has only contemporary value, contemporary expression.

The natural needs of a human being are basic: food, clothing and shelter. You must either work for them or be given them by somebody. If these are your only needs they are not very difficult to fulfill. To deny yourself the basic needs is not a sign of spirituality. But to require more than food, clothing and shelter is a neurotic state of mind.

Is not sex a basic human requirement? Sex is dependent upon thought. In the natural state, there is no build-up of thought. Without that build-up sex is impossible. The body normally is a very peaceful organism and then you subject it to this tremendous tension and release which feels pleasurable to you. Actually, it is painful to the body. But through suppression or attempts at sublimation of sex you will never come into this state.

As long as you think of God you will have thoughts of sex. Ask any religious seeker you may know who practices celibacy whether he doesn't dream of women at night. Why do you weave so many taboos and ideas around this? Why do you destroy the joy of sex? Not that I am advocating indulgence or promiscuity but through abstinence and continence you will never achieve a thing.

There must be a living contact. There are no images here. There is no room for them. The sensory apparatus is completely occupied with the things I am looking at now. And so, if you are totally tuned in to the sensory activity, there is no room for fears about who will feed you tomorrow or for speculation about God, truth and reality. This is not a state of omniscience wherein all of man's eternal questions are answered, rather a state in which the questioning has stopped. It has stopped because those questions have no relation to the way the organism is functioning, and the way the organism is functioning leaves no room for those questions.

The body has an extraordinary mechanism for renewing itself. This is necessary because the senses in the natural state are functioning at the peak of their sensitivity all the time. So when the senses become tired the body goes through death. This is real physical death not some mental state. It can happen one or more times a day. You do not decide to go through this death. It descends upon you.

It feels, at first, as if you have been given an anaesthetic. The senses become increasingly dull, the heartbeat slows, the feet and hands become ice cold and the whole body becomes stiff like a corpse. Energy flows from all over the body towards some point. It happens differently every time. The stream of thoughts continues but there is no reading of the thoughts. At the end of this period you conk out. The stream of thought is cut. There is no way of knowing how long that cut lasts.

There is nothing you can say about that time of being conked out. That can never become part of your conscious existence or conscious thinking. You don't know what brings you back from death. If you had any will at that moment you could decide not to come back. When the conking out is over, the stream of thought picks up exactly where it left off. The dullness ends and clarity returns. The body feels very stiff then slowly it begins to move of its own accord, limbering itself up. It is an extraordinary movement. Those who have observed my body moving say it looks like the motions of a newly born baby. This conking out gives a total renewal of the senses, glands and nervous system. After it, they function at the peak of their sensitivity.

Life is action. Questioning your actions is destroying the expression of life. A person who lets life act in its own way without the protective movement of thought has no self to defend. What is keeping you from being in your natural state? You are constantly moving away from yourself. You want to be happy either permanently or at least for this moment. You are dissatisfied with your everyday experiences and so you want some new ones. You want to perfect yourself, to change yourself. You are reaching out, trying to be something other than what you are. It is this that is taking you away from yourself.

Society has put before you the ideal of a perfect man. No matter in which culture you were born, you have scriptural doctrines and traditions handed down to you to tell you how to behave. You are told that through due practice you can even eventually come into the state attained by the sages and saints, and so you try to control your behavior, to control your thoughts, to be something unnatural. Your effort to control life has created a secondary movement of thought within you which you call the self.

This movement of thought within you is parallel to the movement of life but isolated from it. It can never touch life. You are a living creature yet you lead your entire life within the realm of this isolated, parallel movement of thought. You cut yourself off from life. That is something very unnatural. The natural state is not a thoughtless state. That is one of the greatest hoaxes perpetrated for thousands of years. You will never be without thought. Being able to think is necessary to survive but in this state thought stops choking you. It falls into its natural rhythm.

This is the crux of the whole problem. The one that is looking at what you call the self is the self. It is creating an illusory division of itself into subject and object, and through this division it is continuing. This is the divisive nature that is operating in you, in your consciousness. Continuity of its existence is all that interests it. As long as you want to understand yourself or to change yourself into something spiritual, into something holy, beautiful or marvelous, you will continue. If you do not want to do anything about it, it is not there. It's gone.

Through thinking you cannot understand a thing. You are translating what I am saying in terms of the knowledge you already have just as you translate everything else, because you want to get something out of it. When you stop doing that, what is there is what I am describing. The absence of what you are doing—trying to understand or trying to change yourself—is the state of being that I am describing. Because you are not interested in the everyday things and happenings around you, you have invented the beyond, timelessness, God, truth, reality, enlightenment or whatever, and search for it.

There may not be any ultimate truth. You don't know a thing about it. Whatever you know is what you have been told, what you have heard, and you are projecting that information. What you call something is determined by the learning you have about it, and whatever knowledge you have about it is exactly what you will experience. The knowledge creates the experience and the experience then strengthens the knowledge. What you know can never be ultimate reality.

In the natural state the movement of self is absent. The absence of this movement probably is the beyond but that can never be experienced by you. It is when the you is not there. The moment you translate, the you is there. You look at something and recognize it. Thought interferes with the sensation by translating. You are either thinking about something which is totally unrelated to the way the senses are functioning at the moment or else labeling. That is all that is there. The word separates you from what you are looking at, thereby creating the you. Otherwise, there is no space between the two.

Every time a thought is born, you are born. When the thought is gone, you are gone. But the you does not let the thought go and what gives continuity to this you is the thinking. Actually, there is no permanent entity in you, no totality of all your thoughts and experiences. You think that there is somebody who is thinking your thoughts, somebody who is feeling your feelings. That's the illusion. I can say it is an illusion but it is not an illusion to you.

Your emotions are more complex but it is the same process. There is a sensation in you and you name it. This brings into existence the one who is translating this sensation. Self is nothing but a word. This labeling is only necessary when you must communicate. You think the thoughts of your society, feel the feelings of your society and experience the experiences of your society. There is no new experience. So all that any man has ever thought or felt must go out of your system. And you are the product of all that knowledge. That's all you are.

7

BELIEF

Q: Mr. U.G. Krishnamurti, since you don't believe in traditions, you don't believe in mind, and you don't believe in the existence of soul or any so-called internal human being, let me start with the first question. Why do you follow the tradition of keeping a name? Why do you carry a name? Why do you identify yourself as U.G. Krishnamurti? Because this is also part of a tradition.

U.G.: Yes, that this true. But you could give me a prisoner number. And many of the people who think they are enlightened people and those who give up, become Sannyasins, they have a new name. What actually happens when you don't use the name that is given to us to by our parents, it that you have to develop a new kind of identity there. So what is important to us is to maintain the identity.

When people ask me the question "What's your name?" it takes a little time for the computer to come up with the name U.G.

Krishnamurti. Since Krishnamurti is such a common name and there were so many Krishnamurti's living at the time when I lived in Adyar, we all decided to use the initials U.G. So that is why everybody calls me U.G. My children call me U.G.

Q: But you see, naming is a part of a very complicated tradition. Krishnamurti itself, you know, denotes many things. It denotes Krishna, it denotes its incarnation, it denotes so many things. Why do you keep that name? Why haven't you changed it?

U.G.: As I said a while ago it doesn't make any difference whether I call myself Krishnamurti or use a number. Now it's a lot easier for these computers to handle numbers than with names. So you have a bank account with a number, home address with a number, a telephone number. It's a lot easier for the computer here to deal with the numbers than with the names given to us.

And to me the tradition is nothing but unwillingness on our part to change with the changing things. Things are changing constantly, and we are not ready to change and move along with the change in the things in our life. So we call it tradition and cover it up to feel that we are all very traditional people. Then the story begins. You have to create an identity there again with the number instrument. So it doesn't really matter whether I call myself Krishnamurti, 48592 or any other number.

Q: Fine. It seems you do not believe in philosophy, or you do not agree with the meaning of the world philosophy. And you say that you do not have anything to give, anything to convey. In that sense what should others call you? A philosopher? A revolutionary? A thinker or what? What would you like yourself to be termed as?

U.G.: No, I have the same problem. They asked me the question "Who the hell are you?" So to satisfy them I tell them that I'm a philosopher of some sort. You know the meaning of the word philosopher is a lover of wisdom.

I'm the luckiest man that has found that the totality of wisdom has a stranglehold on the people, and we are brainwashed to believe there is something extraordinary about the totality of wisdom that is passed down to us from generation to generation. We have been brainwashed for centuries to hold on to the great wisdom traditions that have been passed on to us from generation to generation. Because if you change your diet you think you will die. That's one of the reasons why we given tremendous importance to wisdom. As far as I'm concerned it doesn't mean a thing to me.

So people ask me "Who the hell are you?" I say that I am a philosopher of some sort. And I always have this problem when I go on radio programs like this or on television. They ask me the questions "Who are you?" or "Why the hell are you here?" "You have nothing to offer the individuals or the world at large."

My interest is to put across something which has happened to me, something extraordinary, and I know well that this is something which cannot be shared with others because it is not something...

Q: When did this happen?

U.G.: I do not know. I wish I knew. But something hit me.

Q: Why did it happen?

U.G.: Because all my life I wanted to discover the self, find out the self, and the demand to bring about a change in me obsessed me for my formative years, and later on this question haunted me.

Q: But self sounds something like a soul. You're talking about something eternal, aren't you?

U.G.: No, nothing. You know the meaning of the word self is spirit. It's a Latin word. I don't want to deal with the etymological meaning of the word.

Q: Spiritual doesn't mean the body.

U.G.: There is nothing there other than this physical organism functioning with an extraordinary intelligence of its own. So if anybody who is interested in finding out if there is any spirit, if there is any soul, if there is a mind, if there is a psyche. It doesn't matter what name you use or if there is an identity there, if there is an "I" there.

How do we go about it? The only way to go about it is you have to free yourself from everything everybody has said about this before. What you see there is created by you. So the demand to fit ourselves in a value system created by our culture is the one that is sapping out a tremendous amount of energy. And so we are not able to deal with the living problems. The demand to fit ourselves into the value system is the cause of man's tragedy. And there is no point in replacing one value system with another value system. That is what you call revolution. That is what you call by fancy names. But revolution, to put it in my own favorite way, is to replace one value system with another value system. And so the question...

Q: But value is a very subjective term. Whatever you are saying can be termed as a value system itself.

U.G.: I don't think they can make anything out of this and turn this into a model. That is why I am asking people, for goodness sake, don't turn me into a model.

Q: Can I term you as a follower or as a proponent of Charva philosophy or Larva philosophy. It's a very old philosophical system that used to be in India.

U.G.: That is not an appropriate way of caging me into...I don't recommend that kind of a thing to the people. Because everything we are doing is a pleasure movement. Even the beauty you are interested in, the music you are interested in, is nothing but a pleasure movement. So I'm not against a pleasure movement at all. I'm not against anybody saying anything.

What I'm interested in doing is, to use my favorite phrases, to spotlight it and focus it, for them to get the hang of what I am trying to say. What I am trying to say is a very simple thing. There is no way you can figure it out. It's not that I'm trying to mystify this and make it difficult for people to get the hang of what I am trying to say.

I want to leave those listeners, the viewers, and those who come to see me, with this impossibility of figuring out what I am trying to put across. And so in that situation something extraordinary can happen to the individual. You'd be surprised to find out that once this stranglehold of everything that is taught to us, everything that we felt, everything that we experienced before, cannot manipulate these bodies, cannot force the actions to fit into a particular pattern or particular value system.

The whole value system is born out of the assumption that we have great spiritual teachers, and we have turned them into models. So the whole energy is consumed by that demand and our effort to fit ourselves to become copies of those models. So we don't have the guts, we don't have the courage to brush them aside.

There is no way you can brush them aside, no way you can free yourself from belief without replacing that belief with another belief. So belief is not actually a thing that is there. What is there is only a believer. And the believer thinks that he believes in something, so he separates the two. That is a very comforting thing for one who says that I believe in this or that.

So the belief is the most important thing. If the belief comes to an end the you as you know yourself, and the you as you experience yourself, also comes to an end. What you will be left with is anybody's guess. And you have no way of finding out what you are left with. But you just leave that alone to function with an extraordinary intelligent, alertness, alacrity. You are not any more interested in forcing yourself to be put into a value system. At the same time you do not become a rebel. You are not even a rebel without a cause, you are not a revolutionary—you are not any of those things. You are not in conflict with the society you are functioning in. Then it is possible for us to function sanely and intelligently.

Q: This sort-of anarchic description you have just given—do you call it enlightenment. Would you like to term it as enlightenment?

U.G.: I wouldn't use any of those names to describe…

Q: Is it a vacuum? What is it?

U.G.: If you say it's a vacuum it ceases to be a vacuum. If I may define it in my own particular and peculiar way, I would say it is a state of being and not a state of doing. An anarchist, if there is one in this world, would never destroy anything because if he tries to destroy the world around him he's also destroying himself. So anarchy is not the right word to use. But I maintain that if there is a state of anarchy, it is a state of being and not a state of doing. No action is born out of this state of anarchy. You will never be an anarchist to destroy anything because he cannot separate himself from the world around him.

Q: Do you believe in some sort of morality? Is there any place of morality in your system of thinking?

U.G.: When once you are not caught up within the right and wrong, good and bad, moral and immoral…

Q: How do you define good and bad, moral and immoral?

U.G.: They are all definitions given to us by our culture, you see? So we are all the time…

Q: And you would disregard culture. Would you re-define it then?

U.G.: What is the point in redefining it if you become another culture, and the whole cultural story will start all over again? You know, as a matter of fact, somebody asked me a question in one of those television interviews in India: "How do you want us to remember you 500 years after you're gone?" Why the hell do you want to remember me 500 years after I am dead and gone?

Q: That's a very large scale. What I am worried about is how a son, a mother, a father, a brother should behave towards each other. Do you believe in some sort of social morality or not?

U.G.: No, it's not question of belief. It doesn't operate in the lives of the people. We just talk about all those things. That's all. It doesn't operate in the lives of those people.

Q: No, if you are asking people to give away their cultural beliefs altogether...

U.G.: I am not asking them to give up their cultural beliefs. I'm not asking them to do anything. I want you to understand that what you believe in is not operating in your life. I found this in my own way—that the spiritual teachers and their lives would never be put together. There was a tremendous dichotomy, if I may use that nice-sounding word...

Q: Hypocrisy.

U.G.: I didn't want to use the word hypocrisy. Why is there this dichotomy in the lives of people? What they are saying is one thing, what they are doing is totally unrelated to what they are claiming to be. So there must be something wrong. This was my only obsession.

Q: No, but that is a reflection of our capacity because we always try to become ideals. We always try to follow the ideals but we cannot because we have human limitations.

U.G.: That is true. That is the hope we have, the hope that is created by our culture, that one day you are going to be a wonderful person. So when? So you are going to be free from all this 10 years from now, 20 years, and there comes a time when you die, if I may use that word. You invent a thing called reincarnation, and life after death goes on and on and on. Until then I remain what I am.

Q: No, but without hope one ceases to live anyway. I mean life becomes absolutely endless.

U.G.: Not at all. Without hope it is something extraordinary. The nature of that life is something which cannot be imagined.

Q: Do you in any case believe the karma theory, cause and effect, the principle of causality?

U.G.: You see, the word karma in Sanskrit means action. Any action that is born out of thought is destructive. Is there any action called a spontaneous action, pure action, outside the field of cause-and-effect? This is something which you will never know. Because the thought is operating in the field of cause and effect, and it has invented that cause is the effect and effect is the cause; and all that philosophical, metaphysical discussions that go on day after day, day after day. It's very interesting to listen to, but the cause and effect relationship is what you are all the time trying to relate and establish a relationship between.

But every event in life is an independent event. So you have to link up those two and create a story. This is "me". The only way you can create the story of your own life for yourself and others is to relate the two and tell how you can link up cause and effect relationship and tell a story about yourself and others.

Q: It is a basic physical principle. Every action creates a reaction.

U.G.: Not at all. Every event is an independent event. And we think that there cannot be any action...

Q: There is no correlation between two events?

U.G.: No, each event is an independent event.

Q: That means it's a Buddhist philosophy.

U.G.: I don't know what it is. Then if there is no relationship between the two you think that it's going to be a very chaotic way of living. I assure you that it is not going to be a chaotic way of living.

Q: Buddhist philosophy says: every moment ceases to be in itself.

U.G.: They have created a tremendous metaphysics, don't forget that.

Q: That was in reaction to Indian metaphysics.

U.G.: Whatever it is you cannot say there is a void there, that there is a *sunyata* there. So that is the reason why I don't accept the negative approach also. The negative approach is adopted by us because the positive approach to reach our goals has failed, and so we have invented a thing called a negative approach. But the negative approach is still related to the goal. Whatever is the goal—to be in a state of sunyata, to be an enlightened man, to be this or that, to be happy all the time.

So what anybody and everybody is interested in is one basic thing: how to be happy without one moment of unhappiness. I always repeat *ad nauseam*, if I may use that high-sounding phrase, to have pleasure without pain. So every sensation has a limited life. A span of life, you see? The demand to keep that particular sensation, which you call happiness, to last longer than its natural duration of life is the one that is causing all the unhappiness and pain.

This physical body is interested in maintaining its sensitivity. The more you try to keep the sensation of pleasure or the sensation of happiness to last longer you become an unhappy individual. So all those people are telling you: "I have a way to make you feel happy forever. To have pleasure without pain."

There is no way you can be happy without one moment of unhappiness. I tell people that I really do not know what happiness is in life, so I can never, never be unhappy. People ask me "Are you bored?" At no time I feel that there is something more interesting, more purposeful, more meaningful to do than what I am actually doing. So there is no such thing as boredom at all.

I am now talking and my interest is to see that I am in no way trying to influence you or trying to change your point of view or the point of the view of the people out there who are listening or not listening. So just to say things exactly the way they are, not the way I feel, not the way I think they should be. There is no point of view here.

You know the conversation between two persons is always to influence you, to change your point of view. I am not interested in changing your point of view, and there is no way you can change my point of view. So, in most cases, the dialogues and the conversations become meaningless to me, and ultimately in the final analysis, if I may say it so, it is a monologue.

Q: No, but it seems you are challenging the whole linguistic behavior in self, if I may say so. If you talk about the modern concept of linguistic philosophy, whatever you are saying, whatever phrases you are using, have a very strong cultural and social connotation. Would you like to challenge that?

U.G.: I am using that language to find out the absurdity of the individual to use language, to use logic, rationality and the knowledge he has to feel superior; to feel that he is a logical man, that he is a rational man and that he knows a lot more than I do. So that gives the feeling of goodness—that you know more than I do.

When I was a student in university, they were considered to be great professors. I used to tell myself: that fellow has read ten books; I have read only one book. So he's not honest enough, decent enough to admit to the students the source of his information. So why the hell do I have to listen to him?

I would walk out of the class; if I am interested in studying something I can get the same information from the books that he's reading. So he has read 20 books and I have read only one. He's a brilliant orator because he has practiced this art of elocution all his life; he is considered to be one of the greatest orators of our times. So how do I become the orator? Why I want to be an orator is altogether a different story. So that was all that I was interested in. What is it that he has that I don't have?

Whatever I see here is the opposite of what I wanted to be. So this is me. And why am I not enlightened? Because you should be enlightened; you are not happy because you should be happy. And what gives me happiness? If I get what I want I feel happy. If I don't get what I want I'm unhappy. So is there any such a thing as happiness at all? If you can get whatever you want then the question of unhappiness is not of relevance. But we have not succeeded in having one without the other: to be happy always without a moment of unhappiness.

So it is not a question of settling for or accepting the fact of the reality that you cannot always be happy, and that you have to settle for and accept the reality that you can be happy for some time and unhappy some other time.

Q: One basic purpose of ethics and morality is how to deal with others. How would you define that purpose?

U.G.: I will not do anything that will harm others because I am not separate from others.

Q: You believe in the old Indian ethical saying: [foreign language]?

U.G.: No, no. I don't even know what it means. Hurting my fellow being…

Q: It means don't do those things to others which you do not like to be done to you.

U.G.: Not at all. It is not that. It physically hurts me. I am never, never impressed by or affected by the psychological problems of the people. And once you are freed from the psychological info, you realize that what this *is* affected by is what is happening around you—the physical thing that is happening around you. If there is something that I can do to that individual who is suffering I will do it.

Q: Whatever you are saying so far can be interpreted in terms of basic biological or scientific facts. Scientists who deal in biology or scientists who deal in physical science can say all these things. What special you are conveying or saying? And what you would like to term yourself as?

U.G.: Well, some of those scientists come to see me for their own reasons. They tell me what I am saying is true, but they want to believe that I am wrong. The other thing is, they are all theorists. The scientist is just a metaphysician discussing everlastingly the things which do not operate in their lives.

Q: No, for example, you are talking about sensual stimulus which is a physical trait.

U.G.: But it is not translated into sensual activity at all. Because there is no space between the stimulus and the response. They can take me to a laboratory and do some experiments and hit me here and say this is the response to the stimulus. But actually and factually there is no way you can separate the two things. I do not use some metaphysical knowledge or religious stuff that is passed down to me. Actually and factually there is no space between the stimulus and response.

Q: That means you are saying something more than biological facts.

U.G.: I don't know. I don't claim. This is what I have found. This body is functioning with an extraordinary intelligence of its own, and whether it fits into their theories or not is not my interest. They can reject the whole thing and say its absolute rubbish.

Q: Does the world end with our body?

U.G.: The world doesn't exist for you even now. It is just an idea. What you are trying to experience, the world you are referring to is only through the help of the knowledge that is given to us. That's all. So you cannot experience...

Q: That means that the idea of world is false.

U.G.: I am not talking of the world as an illusion or a *Maya*. It is not my philosophy professors that taught me this. *Maya* means to measure. My grandmother, who was practically illiterate, told me, "Look here, *Maya* means to measure." This is the meaning of the word Maya.

There must be a point there, and in relationship with that you experience things, the world around you. So anything you experience from that point is an illusion, but the world is not an illusion. If somebody comes with a gun and he wants to shoot you what would you do? I don't know what I would do. Probably I will kill him or I will run away or I will do everything possible to protect myself. I cannot visualize what I would do in a given situation at all. So it does mean that I say that the world is an illusion but there is no way you can experience the reality of anything without using the knowledge that is given to us either by the metaphysicians or by the scientists. We all admire the scientists because their discoveries have resulted in tremendous technology, which helps us to function in this world most comfortably. That's all that they can do for us. But the same thing can be used to destroy the very thing we are trying to protect.

Q: Last question.

U.G.: Yes, sir.

Q: Generally, the purpose of philosophy is to tell people why they should do good things because they need to know, they need to have some sort of logic to do good things. Since you do not believe in philosophy, you do not believe in any cultural system. Tell me why people should do good things.

U.G.: I don't see any adequate reason why they should do anything good. While they are only concerned about doing good things, they are, all the time, doing bad things. And what they are left with is this misery of wanting to do good things. Wanting.

Q: No, you don't want them to do good things or think about good things.

U.G.: Because there are no good things and bad things for me. I am perfectly satisfied with the world as it is. The demand to bring about a change isn't there anymore.

Q: No matter how miserable it sounds?

U.G.: I don't see anything miserable there. We are responsible for the misery. Individually, there isn't a damn thing, if I may use that word...

Q: There must be something to...

U.G.: Why do you say there must be something? You see? You do something. What is it that they are doing? They are talking of a new world order, the world in transition, the world from where to where.

Q: You think this world cannot be improved at all?

U.G.: Why should it be different? It can't be any different. We being what we are I don't see any reason, and I don't believe the world can be any different. It has always been the same. I once told a friend of mine that we have not made any tremendous strides. We are not any more different from the caveman who used the jawbone of an ass to kill his neighbor, and now with the help of all these scientists, nuclear physicists, we have destructive weapons to destroy the whole thing that we have created with great care.

8

ANSWER

Wanting and thinking. In the Chinese language they use the same word for wanting and thinking. They're not two different words. So whatever you want, the only way you can achieve whatever you want is through thinking. No other way. Right?

Then if I use thinking as a means to get what I want I have to depend upon somebody else. He is telling you, "This is the way I got whatever I wanted." This is the way you are going to get whatever you want: through thinking. You understand? No you don't understand. Huh?

So anything you want, that want can be fulfilled, achieved only through thinking. So that means I am already dependent on somebody else. There is nothing which you can call your own. No experience is your own. No feeling is your own. No thought is your own. All that is put in there, the shit. And you have to use that to experience, see? The experience of somebody else, to

ANSWER

experience that, you have to use that, there is no other way you can experience anything. Should I stop?

We love suffering and enjoy suffering. Why not? We are living misery, sitting misery, walking misery, and then you die in your misery. There is no way you can free yourself. You may say that I am cynical or pessimistic; that I am this, that or the other. No, sorry, no.

It is really comforting for you to think that you are an optimist and I am a pessimist. And if I say that God is irrelevant, you think that you are a believer in God and I am an atheist. But get this and get this straight. An atheist is still interested in God. He may say that he doesn't believe in God, but by his desire to free others from their belief in God, he becomes a missionary to free you from your belief in God, and you are another kind of a missionary who wants to make people believe in God. So, both are in the same boat.

And the worst situation is when someone calls himself an agnostic. He's sitting on the fence, hoping that one day science will find out if there is a God, and you can jump on that side, or the other side. So that's the worst. Don't trust the agnostics.

The only difference, if there is any difference, between the way you are functioning and the way I am functioning, *if* there is any difference. Take it or leave it. The thought that I am different from you never enters my head. See then suppose you come here, and I never tell myself that I am different from you, you see? So if you ask me a question then I would know that you and I are not functioning in exactly the same way. It is not that the way I am functioning is far superior to yours or something different. But not that, you see. There are no questions of that kind in me. Right? The questions you are asking I have probably asked before. But that is not the point. You can't draw a line between the before and after. My favorite thing to say is that there is only a before and after with washing powder. Washing clothes. Before washing and after washing.

And what is comforting to you is you did all those things; you did sadhana, you did meditation, you did yoga, you listened to J. Krishnamurti, you read all those books, that is only a comforting thought for you, and that gives you hope that one day you will be free from all that and function like me. Not a chance, you see? You cannot be me. Not that I am far superior, that I am unparalleled, unique, nothing of the kind.

As long as you want to be something other than what actually you are, you will be in misery. And you fall for them, they say that I am an enlightened man, that some radical transformation has taken place in me, that you must also function like me. Don't believe all those people at all. Sorry. If you want to, good luck to you. You are not going to get anything from anybody. If I want to learn how to operate a video camera I have to take a few lessons from somebody. If I want to learn how to operate a computer I have to take lessons from them. Through a repetitive process, through trial and error, you master that. In that area *only* it is possible for us to learn something and perfect that through thinking. Perfecting something means a repetitive process.

In the other areas it is just not possible. So the thought that I am different from you never, never enters my head. Only if you ask

ANSWER

me the question, "Why is he asking those questions?" "Why doesn't he accept what I am saying?" All the questions are born out of the answers you already have. If you don't have any answers there are no questions. I have very often emphasized, over-emphasized, *this*: that you're not interested in the answers at all. You see, I am not giving you any answers at all. Nobody is giving any answers. What you are interested in is to get answer so that you can maintain the continuity of the answers you already have. Otherwise there wouldn't be any questions. Actually, if there is any answer, the answer is put into the question you're asking. The fact that you're asking questions again and again means that that is not the answer.

So the next thing is: the questioner and the question are one and the same. There is no questioner who is asking the questions. So if the question comes to an end the questioner automatically comes to an end. The questioner is the answer. You ask the question about your belief in God, for example. Why are you still asking the question "Does God exist?" What for? That means you are not certain. If you are certain you will become a visionary, you will become a Pope, you will run a church, right? The fact that you are asking questions means that you are not certain of the answers that are there in you which are put there by your conscience, society, or whatever you want to call it. So if there any answer to the question, the question should come to an end. Since the question is not separate from the questioner, the questioner comes to an end. You are not interested in that. You cannot be interested in that at all. Because all the questions are the variations of the same question. One question. When it comes to an end the questioner comes to an end, and along with it the whole thing is finished.

You want to keep the questioner going, and all questions are the variations of the same question.